# AN AMERICAN ODYSSEY

## *The Bob Mathias Story*

by
Bob Mathias
and Robert Mendes

SPORTS PUBLISHING L.L.C.
SportsPublishingLLC.com

Director of production: Susan M. Moyer
Dustjacket and photo insert design: Terry Neutz Hayden
Proofreader: Christopher Stolle


ISBN:
hardcover: 1-58382-022-1
softcover: 1-58261-355-9


**SPORTS PUBLISHING L.L.C.**
www.sportspublishingllc.com

Printed in the United States.

*This book is dedicated with love to the memory of Haven, Jordan and Elijah Halstead, who should have grown up to read about their grandfather, but who never will.*

—————————————————

# Contents

# Acknowledgments

The authors would be remiss if they did not acknowledge the valuable contributions of the following:

*Gwen Mathias*—a loving inspiration, a perfect companion and, perhaps, the most patient person in the world.

Tulare Museum's *Ellen Gorelick* and *Chris Harrell* who knew where everything was when we wanted it. Their willingness to help and their cooperation were deeply appreciated.

*Frank Zarnowski*—whose knowledge of the decathlon is encyclopedic and whose understanding of the event is greater than anyone's on earth. Without Zeke's willingness to share his wealth of information, this book could perhaps not have been written.

My brother—*Eugene Mathias,* who remembered things about me even I had forgotten.

My brother—*Jimmy Mathias* and sister *Patricia Guererro* for their valuable contributions to the book and especially for being my brother and sister.

*Bob Hoegh*—Another font of wisdom and source of information. No one ever had a better friend.

*Mike Harrigan*—who provided information we thought was lost forever. The same information provided to us was provided by Mike for the late James Michener's book, *Sport in America*, but, because of political considerations at the time, was attributed to an "Unknown author." We are pleased to remove Mike's cloak of anonymity and thank him publicly.

*Keith Jura*—who was at lunch with us when we first agreed to write this book.

*Tom Bast*—of Sports Publishing Inc. who was there when we needed him.

*Larry Bortstein*, writer for the *Orange County Register*, former *Presidents Gerald Ford* and *George Bush*, and the many others whose knowledge and recollections helped the authors make this book less dreary than it might have been.

Last but certainly far from least, *Bette Mendes*, a great wife, a diligent proofreader and a willing critic.

# Foreword

_____

*by Gerald R. Ford*

As a former athlete, I was always a supporter and, in some cases, even a hero-worshipper of Olympic gold medallists.

As Republican Leader of the House of Representatives in 1966, it meant a great deal to me personally to have an honest-to-God Olympic hero be elected to join the Republican ranks.

My first impression of Bob Mathias was less of him as a person but rather the effect he had on people meeting him for the first time. He was very attractive in appearance and a low-key campaigner. You were initially attracted by his name, his presence and appearance, but, once you got to know him, it was his sound judgment that was very impressive.

Bob and I always worked well together, and it was very helpful that we'd had major competition backgrounds in our youth. It created an easy relationship for us. I think even before we met, we had sort of an understanding that there would be some sort of rapport between us.

—Gerald R. Ford
*38th President of the United States*
*All-American center, University of Michigan*

# *Preface*

---

*The 17-year-old boy knows he will live forever.*
*The man, 50 years later, knows better.*

In 1948, the world made a big deal out of a 17-year-old kid winning a gold medal in the Olympic Decathlon, then an even bigger deal when he came back four years later to repeat. I'm Bob Mathias, once that 17-year-old kid, once impervious to injury, to aging, to the frailties of man . . . once immortal.

And then one day, not so immortal.

Just scared.

Lying in a bed at the Stanford University Medical Center; terrified that my mortality was upon me.


My wife Gwen and I had been at the 1996 Olympics in Atlanta when I noticed one night at dinner I was having trouble swallowing. I didn't think much about it, until after a few days the problem didn't seem to be going away.

When the Olympics ended, we made a brief trip to Vermont to attend a meeting, stopped off at friends in North Carolina, and visited Gwen's family in Arkansas. Then, on August 20, we were back home in Fresno, California.

The next day, I visited a local doctor.

When a doctor looks into your throat and utters the word "biopsy," you get a feeling like nothing you've ever experienced. I actually felt a chill run into my scalp. He scheduled the biopsy for the following week. Driving home, I thought to myself: "Why me? I've never even had a cigarette in my mouth . . . . "

When I got home, I called my brother Eugene, who is a retired doctor. I told him my symptoms and what my doctor had said.

"A week!? Hell, you can't wait a week for something like this," Gene said. "Don't go away, I'll call you right back."

That was not the reaction I had hoped for from Gene. I was looking for him to say something offhanded like: "Don't make this into a big deal. It's probably nothing." His obvious sense of urgency wasn't the least bit comforting.

Twenty minutes later, he called back and told me to get my butt up to Palo Alto, where a Dr. Fee was waiting for me.

I was nervous, anxious and scared, but I couldn't help laughing: "Dr. Fee!?"

Within an hour, Gwen and I were headed north to get a second opinion from Dr. Willard Fee, Chairman of the Otolaryngology Division at the Stanford University Medical Center.

He did an on-the-spot biopsy and diagnosed a squamous cell carcinoma about the size of a quarter, deep in my throat. He admitted me to the medical center that afternoon and told me there were two possible treatments. One was surgery, which carried a virtual certainty of the loss of a vocal chord. The other was chemotherapy and radiation, a lengthy procedure, guaranteed to make me deathly ill for weeks at a time. Some choice. Dr. Fee recommended the latter, and, after another conversation with Gene, I opted for the chemo.

I've heard chemotherapy compared to seasickness. Believe me, seasickness would be a welcome relief. What chemotherapy does is kill off the cancerous cells in your body. Unfortunately, it kills off nearly everything else as well, including those microorganisms that help you digest your food.

During 20 days of chemotherapy I was unable to eat anything solid, lost 55 pounds, and was sick all the time. But when I considered the alternative, I figured I was doing OK.

It was some time around then that Gwen said: "You've got stories to tell that no one in the world knows. Maybe you should think about writing a book?"

**Gwen Mathias:**

*Bob is one of the most modest men you will ever meet. I'm not just saying that because he's my husband. Our marriage is the second one for both of us, so I wasn't with him during his days as an Olympic athlete or as a congressman. If someone hadn't told me about him, I would never have known how famous he was. He certainly never would have.*

*I'm sure there are stories about him that even I still don't know, so maybe we can all learn about this man Bob Mathias together.*

So, having finally accepted my mortality, I'll take Gwen's advice and tell about those parts of my life that might be interesting.

All in all, it's been a terrific life, and, for the most part, good things kept happening to me. But like anyone, I had some low points, too. Before I was ready to end my career as an amateur athlete, the AAU ended it for me, because I had committed the sin of accepting money to play myself in the movie, *The Bob Mathias Story*. An athlete accepting *money*, can you imagine?

So I pursued a career in the movies for awhile, where I met some fascinating people, whom I'll tell you about.

I will also share my recollections of four terms in the U.S. Congress. Having spent eight years in the nation's capital in the '60s and '70s (can you say *Watergate?*) was as tumultuous as it gets.

But the thing that seems—still—to define my life is having won the Olympic decathlon twice in a row. I never thought of it as such a big deal, but since the only other person who's ever done it— Daley Thompson from England—won in 1980 when the Americans boycotted the Olympics and in 1984 when the Soviets didn't attend, maybe it was. Big deal or not, I can tell you it certainly wasn't as financially rewarding as it would be today.

I also operated a boys camp in the Sierra Nevada Mountains for many years; so, as you can see, I could never stick with one career.

**Frank Zarnowski (Leading international authority on the decathlon):**

*"Bob's is typical of the decathlon mind-set. These guys are so good at so many things they can't stick with just one event like, say, the 100 meters or the pole vault. They have to extend themselves to see how many worlds they can conquer. Apparently it carries over into other aspects of their lives, too."*

So here I am, Mathias the athlete, Mathias the actor, Mathias the congressman, Mathias the businessman, and even some other careers that slipped in over the years.

I hope I have some interesting stories to tell you about my worlds, but don't expect this little jog around the track to be all fun. I also intend to talk about a system that seems to have lost touch with reality; a system that offers seven-figure salaries to second-string ballplayers; that slaps them on the wrist for committing crimes against their fellow man (and woman) and encourages them to act like superheroes in front of the TV camera simply for doing their job. Don't you just *love* the end zone and sack dances?

I'll collect my thoughts, look over my shoulder at some memories, peer into the future a little and maybe even tweak some people.

Another thing I'd like to do in this book, is answer some questions I've been asked over the years. The most obvious is one that comes up more and more lately. "Do I resent the dollars being paid to today's athletes—professional *and amateur?*"

I'll answer that one now. The answer is no, I don't resent it. Sure, if I had been born, say, 30 years later, perhaps by my mid-20s I could have made enough money so that I never would need to work again. But if I had, I might have missed out on all those careers and other experiences that were, themselves, highly rewarding.

I'm sure every generation remembers its youth as *The Good Old Days,* but there actually is truth in that. When I look back at my youth, I believe the world was a simpler, happier place, at least that's the way it seemed. I think it took less to make us happier because there *was* less.

The boyhood happiness we knew in the '30s and '40s was happiness that money couldn't buy, and I'll try to tell you about it. Today's athletes have more material things than we ever could have imagined, but are they happy? I wonder.

When I read about an athlete beating his wife or raping his date or driving under the influence or being picked up with drugs—when I see that the *Los Angeles Times* now has a part of its Sports section called "Jurisprudence," given over to details of athletes' legal transgressions, I wonder. I really wonder.

During the Atlanta Olympics, I remember experiencing mixed feelings as the Dream Team pranced to another 30-point victory. Sure, it was great that my country was on the verge of another gold medal, but on a different level, I found myself brooding over what has happened to the Olympics and to sports in general. I asked myself four questions that night that might seem a little corny. However, I'll lay them out for you, since, to some degree, they are the basis for this book.

1.  What has happened to the joy of competing for the sake of competing?
2.  Is there relevance only in winning?
3.  Must everything have a huge financial reward to be meaningful?
4.  Why does the sports section read like the police report?

This is not to imply that all is wrong in sports. On the contrary, much is right and wonderful. More people are competing; women, in particular have stormed upon the sports scene as some of the best athletes pound-for-pound the world has ever seen. Hundreds of thousands of people are out in the streets or in gyms running or bicycling or staying healthy and getting in shape in many different ways.

On the fiftieth anniversary of my first gold medal, I think I have something meaningful to say about today's sports and athletes and our way of life in general.

And the incredible changes we've seen . . . .

I would understand if today's athletes would not believe how things used to be. By today's standards, we did everything wrong. We ate the wrong foods and wore the wrong shoes. Our training methods were ludicrous, and our equipment was pathetic.

And the ethics . . .

*O Tempores; O Mores*

Oh the times; oh the customs!

# CHAPTER *1*

# Did You Really Run on Cinders?

## Who Wants to Hear a Story?

**Okay kids, climb up on Uncle Bob's knee,** and I'll tell you about the olden days—back when we wore our letter sweaters to the malt shop on Friday night; when a nickel bag referred to licorice, and when athletes went to classes, studied, and even graduated. Now, you stop that snickering.

The story starts way back in 1930, when a man named Herbert Hoover was living on Pennsylvania Avenue, and the country was in the Great Depression. The University of Pittsburgh started out the year by destroying Cal, 47-14 in the Rose Bowl. Americans were humming "I Got Rhythm," and movie houses were showing Wallace Beery in "The Big House" and Marlene Dietrich in "Blue Angel." The Oscar for Best Picture went to "All Quiet on the Western Front."

Meanwhile, on America's western front, in the tiny farm town of Tulare, in California's central valley, a wholly unremarkable event took place on November 17. A baby named Robert Bruce was born to Dr. Charles Mathias and his wife Lillian, continuing what they would eventually call the Three-Year Plan. It seems that every three years they added another child. They started in 1927 with my brother Eugene, then I showed up in 1930, then Jimmy in 1933 and finally our sister Patricia in 1936.

Maybe I got my decathlete's need to diversify from our father. He was a general practitioner and treated everything from hangnails to heart attacks. He was a pediatrician, a geriatrician and everything in between. He did surgery and psychology; faith healing and family counseling. He even holds the record for having delivered the most babies in Tulare.

Considering the farm country we lived in, I wouldn't be surprised if he was even pressed into a little veterinary service now and then. Dad didn't always get paid in the coin he would have liked, but then he didn't have to deal with HMOs and insurance companies, either. Given the occupation of most of his patients, though, we always had plenty of fresh fruit, vegetables, milk, eggs, meat— even fresh flowers on the table.

Lillian, our mother, was resident cook, housekeeper, nurse, disciplinarian, and saint. When I weighed in at a hefty nine-and-a-half pounds, she confided to Dad: "Oh, Charles, a girl would have been so nice." She got over her disappointment, eventually had her little girl and became my greatest fan and archivist. The Tulare Historical Museum has an entire section of Bob Mathias memorabilia, all lovingly compiled, categorized, and recorded by Lillian Mathias.

Tulare's population was about 6,000, and increasing rapidly when I was born. A lot of people were moving west hoping to find land or jobs. Many, like my parents, came from Oklahoma and the plains states, which were suffering not only from the Great Depression, but also from the terrible drought so graphically depicted in John Steinbeck's *The Grapes of Wrath*. The newcomers were attracted to the warm weather, the fertile soil, and the beautiful, unspoiled landscape.

My recollections of Tulare are of security, loving warmth and one of the most beautiful places in the world. What a feeling to get up on a winter morning, look out my bedroom window and see the peaks of the distant Sierra Nevada Mountains accumulating snow while our temperature was in the 60s. It fostered an indescribable feeling of well-being.

Tulare is 10 miles south of Visalia, the capital of Tulare County and about 200 miles due north of Los Angeles. But L.A. might as well have been on another planet. It wasn't the sprawling mess it is today, and besides, if we had need for a big city and bright lights . . .hey, we had Fresno just 50 miles to the north.

Today, we would probably be described as a close-knit family. In those days, it was just the norm. Occasionally, my brother Eugene let me hang around with him and his friends—even though they were three years older—so to repay the favor, once in a while I'd let Jimmy tail along with my friends and me.

I have to believe one of the major differences between us growing up in the middle of the century and kids growing up today—whether they're athletes or not—is attitude.

We were just wide-eyed naïfs, and you could sum up our attitude in four words: *"I can do it."*

That thought was drummed into us by our teachers, our coaches and, most important, our parents. I remember my mother and father telling me over and over again: "You can do it, Robert," and not only in a sports context.

"You can pass your history test, Robert."

"You can understand algebra, Robert."

"You can get into Stanford, Robert."

"You can do whatever you put your mind to Robert."

Compare *"I can do it,"* to another four-word phrase; one that's popular today: *"Been there, done that,"* and perhaps it will point to one of the problems with today's *role models.*

The Mathias backyard was like a recreation center. We had a long jump pit, a high bar, and what we called the action bar. It was something my dad rigged up, to which we could attach ropes, swings, and all kind of other apparatus.

It was in that backyard that I had one of the scariest moments of my life. I was about seven, and I was pushing my sister Patricia on the swing. I guess I started pushing a little too vigorously, and she flew off the swing, landed on her head and didn't move. I was convinced I had killed her.

Panicky and on the verge of tears, I ran into the house to get mom, but by the time we got back outside, Patricia was sitting up and crying.

It's been many years since that day, and I've had children and grandchildren of my own, but no feeling I've ever had can match the overpowering sense of relief and joy I felt when I saw Patricia crying. I scooped her in my arms and kept hugging her until she started wriggling to get away from me. "Let me go, Robert," she said.

There were five of us guys who were inseparable: Bob Hoegh, Bob Abercrombie, Dane Sturgeon, Sim Innes, and me. Sim was one of the best athletes I ever knew and won the gold medal in the discus at the 1952 Olympics.

I feel fortunate that Bob Hoegh and I have stayed close friends over all these years and are still as close today as we were as kids. Bob and I went through the growing-up wars together. We met in the seventh grade when his family moved to town, and, although we were separated for years at a time, we never lost touch with each other. He was co-captain of our high school basketball team and defensive end on the football team.

In addition to high school, Bob and I went to Kiskiminetas Prep School together, as well as Stanford.

Bob has spent his life doing something that I think is the highest calling of man—working with boys. He was the football coach at Modesto Junior College and had one of the most rewarding careers of anyone I know.

As I remember my boyhood with my friends, we were always out, jumping and running and *doing*.

I came by it naturally. Dad was a track and football star in high school and was a standout end at the University of Oklahoma, where he and my mom met. Mom grew up in Oklahoma's Osage Territory, where her father kept a general store. My brother Eugene was a great all-around athlete too, but during a football game he suffered a severe concussion that partially paralyzed him for a while, and my dad decided Eugene's football career was over. But Eugene did excel in track and became captain of the Tulare Union High School basketball team in his senior year. At Stanford, he was a member of the golf team.

My younger brother Jimmy was no slouch in track and field, either. He competed at the national level and won the U.S. Army Championship in the discus when he was stationed in Germany. Our sister Patricia was a competitive swimmer—a pretty good one, too.

We probably gave our parents plenty to worry about, but as I think back on our childhood—with my, *ahem*, selective memory— I think we were probably pretty good kids.

Mom and Dad delivered discipline, love, and humor all on the same platter, and we kids always knew where the line not to cross was. Even so, I'm sure Eugene and I drove them crazy once in a while.

I remember there was a family decision (translation: mom and dad decided) that Eugene and I were to wash the dishes each night after dinner. Of all my chores, this was the one I hated the most. I mean—I really hated just standing in front of that stupid sink and doing dishes. After just a single week of the edict, the family inventory of cups, saucers, and dinner plates had diminished alarmingly, but mom and dad persevered. One night, however, laughing and screaming, Eugene and I ended up in a water fight. I was soaked, Gene was soaked, the kitchen floor looked like the deck of the Titanic—and the dishes were still in the sink unwashed. Mom begged dad to let her do the dishes from then on, and Eugene and I didn't complain a bit. We were later accused of setting Mom up, but we'll deny that to the end.

Patricia still teases me about the first time I took her to school. I had mentioned to Miss Margie Shannon, my first grade teacher, that I had a brand new sister. But Miss Shannon had seen mom just the week before at a PTA meeting and noticed nothing to indicate the imminent arrival of another child. I guess I forgot to mention to her that Patricia was adopted. It wasn't the first time that Miss

Shannon had accused me of having an overactive imagination. "Now, Robert..." she would say.

Well, I *did* have a new baby sister, and I could prove it. So the next morning I put a big pillow in my little red wagon and took Patricia to Wilson Grammar School for Show and Tell to validate her existence. If only I had thought to mention to someone that I was taking her . . .

Mom and dad thought she had been kidnapped and were beside themselves. Dad was about to call the cops or the FBI when Mrs. McCourt, one of our neighbors, told mom she had seen us on the way to school. They showed up just as I finished my presentation. I don't remember being punished. I guess after mom and dad's initial scare, they did a lot of head shaking and probably had a pretty good laugh.

One summer, Eugene, Jimmy and I were sent to Camp Tulequoia, a YMCA camp in the Sierra Nevada Mountains. I loved that. I absolutely loved it. That summer and its introduction to the outdoors were so enjoyable, they became an influencing factor that led to a significant chapter in my life. I'll tell you more about Camp Mathias later.

I'm thankful that, as we four siblings grew into adulthood, we remained close. We were able to help one another with life's little problems and were always there for each other. Pat became a hospital administrator. Jimmy was a farmer for awhile, then the maintenance director at Three Rivers School. Eugene, as I mentioned, became a physician.

I always wanted to be a doctor too and, in fact, took a pre-med curriculum in my freshman year at Stanford. However, I got so involved in other things that I just didn't have the time necessary for such rigor.

Mom accused me of being a pack rat. I scoured trash bins for bottle caps (I ended up with over 20,000 of them); traded with other kids for marbles; rutted through empty fields for interesting rocks; and spent my meager allowance on books. If I could carry it, I would collect it. Mom once said that if I had ever become a doctor, I'd probably have bottles of fingers and toes all over the house. Ha! Little did she know that Eugene and I actually did have tonsils, kidney stones, and an appendix hidden in bottles in our room.

Eugene was actually the champion collector of the family, and one of his specialties was birds' eggs. He let me go foraging with him once and challenged me to climb a tall tree in which he had seen a nest. I shinnied up, grabbed two eggs and started to climb down. But going down with one hand wasn't so easy, so I popped the eggs into my mouth. When I came to the lowest branch, I was still four feet from the ground and I had no option but to jump.

*Jump.*

*Bang.*

*Crunch.*

Now I had two fledgling birds fluttering around in my mouth.

*Ptooey.*

From then on, I let Eugene do his egg collecting on his own.

As a young kid, I got a small allowance, but I never really needed money. I had friends. I had family. I had fun all the time. The only things I ever needed money for were an occasional candy bar, which was a nickel, and books, which were a dime. And most books could be gotten at the library for free. Movies were 15 cents, which mom would finance on a Saturday afternoon.

For that 15 cents, we got a double feature, the news, coming attractions, and—what we all went to the movies for in the first place—the Saturday serial! Ah, the cliff-hangers they used to torture us kids with. They'd end a chapter by leaving the good guy tied to the front of a locomotive that had just jumped the tracks and plowed head-on into a mountainside. I would worry about him all week long until it was Saturday again. Then we'd find out he had untied himself just before the collision and was off on his horse going after the guys in the black hats. Hollywood's *Deus ex machina.*

I was lucky. Nearly everything I loved was either free or ridiculously inexpensive. Running and jumping cost nothing, nor did the radio. I loved the Western serials on the radio as well as Don Winslow of the Navy, The Shadow and Tennessee Jed: *"There 'e goes Tennes-*

*see, git 'im. P'tang! Got 'im, da-a-a-id center."* But far and away, my
favorite was Jack Armstrong, the All-American Boy.

It was very seldom that I ever needed extra money, but when I
did, it was pretty easy to come by.  I could do odd jobs—mow
lawns, pick fruit—I could even shovel manure, which wasn't exactly my favorite, but it was always good for a buck or two. I also
helped dad on house calls and actually got pretty good at setting
casts after dad would reduce the fracture.  At one point, I knew the
name of every bone in the body, but not any more.  You know what
they say about growing old: The first thing that goes is your memory
of bone names.

There were always plenty of pets around the house. I raised
mice, rats, and rabbits.  We had canaries, goldfish, parakeets, turtles,
dogs, cats, and even a couple of horses.

Lest I give you the impression that I was that *wonderful* Mathias
boy, I assure you the adjective didn't get applied to me all that often.
When I was six, somehow I got hold of some red paint and decided
our kitchen could use some livening up. I had done the floor, the
door, and two walls before mom came in and, with a screech that
shattered crystal up and down the west coast, ended my career as an
interior decorator.

So I channeled my creativity in other directions and invented
a game. I called it "fling-the-neighbors'-garbage-can-lids-down-the-
alley."  The only point of the game was to beat my previous distance. In fact, after my first Olympic win, Mrs. McCourt bragged
that it was her garbage can lids that gave me my proficiency in the
discus. And who's to say it wasn't so?

When we got older, Eugene used to like to keep me in line by
reminding me: "Listen, kid, you weren't always Bob Mathias."  Let
me explain.

As I approached 11, I began to think that perhaps I was slowly
dying. Whereas in the past I used to jump out of bed and play in
the backyard for an hour or so before school, now I would wake up
in the morning exhausted.  I could just about drag myself through
the day, and I'd come home from school barely able to walk up the

steps to my room.  I caught chicken pox, measles, and whooping cough, one after the other, and my parents were worried because I was always sick.

Dad eventually diagnosed me as being anemic and made me stay in the house and rest. He prescribed iron and vitamin pills, liver, and sleep, exactly as a doctor would do today.  At my present age, being forced to stay home and take it easy doesn't seem all that terrible, but at the time, when I could hear my friends outside playing ball, I thought it was the end of the world.

### Eugene Mathias, (Bob's brother):

*Here's a story about Robert that I have trouble believing myself . . . and I was there!  He had just turned 11 and was unbelievably skinny and frail looking. He was in the early stages of anemia, but none of us knew it at the time. I was with Mr. W. J. Walker, the coach of Wilson Grammar School. Coach Walker was trying to improve my high-jumping technique, and I was stuck just below four feet. Try as I might, I just couldn't clear that height. When coach took me off to the side to demonstrate what I was doing wrong, we caught a movement heading toward the pit. We both turned just in time to see Robert, with absolutely no form, sail over the bar with almost a foot to spare . . . . In only the sixth grade and in the early stages of anemia!*

Those days of illness weren't entirely unproductive.  My mother taught me something that was to prove so valuable to me later, I don't quite know how to assess it. It sounds simple enough, but it was actually pretty complex. She taught me how to relax.

She trained me to lie still and think of different parts of my body, relaxing each one as I thought of it. I'd start with my toes, then my feet, ankles, and so on up my body. Before I knew it, I'd be so totally relaxed that I would fall asleep.

Six years later, on the proverbial dark and stormy night in London's Wembley Stadium, I was able to crawl under a blanket, use mom's relaxation method and sleep between events while my competitors were pacing and worrying and otherwise expending their energy.

### Irv "Moon" Mondschein (three-time national decathlon champion and Bob's 1948 Olympic teammate):

*We guys who had been competing for a while, and knew what we were doing, spent a lot of time jogging around the track between events to keep warm. Meanwhile, Bob would hole up in his blanket and take a little nap. It became kind of his trademark. Anyone looking for "The Kid" knew to look for a lump under a blanket in the middle of the infield.*

While I was sick, mom read to me a lot, especially Will James' westerns. I loved them, and so did the other kids who often gathered around my bed to hear the stories.

Between mom's loving care and dad's doctoring, I recovered completely from the anemia. I ate anything that wouldn't eat me first—steak by the pound, milk by the gallon, peas by the cupful, and anything else put in front of me. Dad strictly forbade me to do anything athletic and, for almost a year, I didn't.

But as I gradually started to feel stronger, I began reverting to my old ways. I never walked when I could run and never went around something I could jump over. As anyone who has suffered an enervating disease like anemia can tell you, you do recover your strength, but only very slowly, and there's always the danger of backsliding.

But I recovered completely, and by the time I got into high school, I was strong as an ox and growing like a weed (and addicted to clichés). When we got older, Gene and I had a routine we used to do for our friends.

*Eugene:* Say Bob, were you always so big and strong?
*Me:* No sir. When I was younger, I was a sick and anemic invalid.
*Eugene:* You don't say. Did you live?
*Me:* Did I live? You should see me now.

I guess that's not nearly as hilarious as we thought when we were back at Tulare Union High. In fact, Gene should be ashamed of himself.

Speaking of high school, those were wonderful years: full of growth and learning for all of us. I think it's so different now for athletes. It makes me sad that the wonder and naiveté seems to have gone out of high school sports—and with it much of the camaraderie. We played for the joy of competing and the exhilaration of winning. We certainly never gave a thought to making a living at it.

Oh, I guess there were some really good high school baseball players who thought that maybe someday if the stars were properly aligned and a plague struck the Pacific Coast League they might stand a chance of making it to the pros.

Speaking of the PCL, I remember an outfielder named Joe DiMaggio playing for the San Francisco Seals because the New York Yankees already had a full outfield. Joe DiMaggio, for God's sake— in the minor leagues! Today, he would have been called up to the majors before his ninth birthday.

Today, some parents of high school kids—and even younger— think they can program their kids to be athletes. Apparently they don't realize a kid has to love a sport before he can excel. I've seen parents berate their kids in front of their friends for not doing well on the Little League field or at a youth soccer game. I get so angry when I see this happening, and I have to wonder what in the world these people are thinking. They don't seem to realize that they're making sports just another assignment.

"Why did you get a D in math?"

"Why didn't you tag up on that fly to right field?"

I'm appalled by stories of girls in their early teens who develop eating disorders as the result of *training* for gymnastics. The problem is the system. The system has taken the joy out of sports and made it a business; a chore in some cases. God forbid a 13-year-old girl gymnast should have a growth spurt the year before the Summer Olympics.

There's one particular case that, thank God, isn't typical but, to a lesser degree, is happening all the time.

I was outraged by the presumption of this father to run his kid's life, on the one hand. On the other hand, I felt profoundly sad for the boy himself. The father was a former USC football star who, from birth, programmed his son's entire life, with the goal being for the kid to play football at USC, excel, then turn pro. The kid allegedly never got to go to McDonald's, took his own health food to other kids' birthday parties and, in general, was permitted no interests outside of football. He was literally programmed for football.

It was well documented in the newspapers how Todd Marinovich self-destructed. He began fulfilling his father's dream by getting a football scholarship to USC, but after two years he rebelled, dropped out of school and declared for the NFL draft. He was drafted by the (then) Los Angeles Raiders and almost immediately became their starting quarterback. But almost as quickly, he came apart with drugs, alcohol, and who knows what else.

There is no doubt in my mind that the boy's behavior pattern was a reflexive mutiny against the pressure his father had put on him. Just think: this was a bright, good-looking kid, and unquestionably a gifted athlete. He could have had four wonderful years of college, possibly a long career in the NFL and been a role model for younger kids. He no doubt was given a ton of money, but money doesn't last forever. So where is he? He has no degree and probably very little real understanding of what life is all about. I'm sure his father is very proud.

Considering the size of Tulare, we turned out some pretty famous people. Bud Zumwalt, whose father was mayor of Tulare, was six years ahead of me, so we didn't exactly pal around together—six years being a whole different generation at that age. But when Bud became Admiral Elmo Zumwalt, Chief of Naval Operations for the United States Navy, I thought about this guy who lived just three doors away and was thrilled that good ol' Bud, who used to chase me down the street, had reached the pinnacle of his field. *"Good for you, Bud,"* I thought. *"And good for Tulare.'*

We also had some pretty good athletes in town. Bob Hoegh was an outstanding all-around athlete who played on the basketball and football teams with me in high school, prep school, and at Stanford. By far, the biggest and strongest, was my friend Sim Innes. When we were juniors, Sim was a 6-foot-3, 200-pound offensive lineman made of iron. He also could throw the discus a mile. We just lived for sports and loved the competition.

While other guys were at dances and dating, Sim and I were out on the track battling tooth and nail for inches on the tape and split seconds on the clock. Reports of UFOs in California's central valley were just Sim and me trying to beat each other's distance in the discus. If it hadn't been for Sim, I might never have achieved much in track and field. There were times when I would watch one of Sim's throws just take off and sail forever. Then, of course, I would have to try to beat it. Sometimes I could; all too often I couldn't. But the point is we were so competitive, we learned at an early age what it is to put out everything you have—and then put out a little more.

Sim died recently, and I miss him dearly.

### Bob Hoegh (Bob's lifelong friend):

*Bob Mathias has no business talking about other athletes. I've seen him do things no person has any right to do. For example, we had a friend on the diving team who spent two months perfecting a one-and-a-half forward flip. One day, at the community pool, he did one for us. Then Bob said to me: "I wonder if I can do that." He got on the board and did an absolutely perfect one-and-a-half —first time out!*

*Another time I marveled at his athletic ability was at a high school track meet. He had this uncanny ability to fall asleep at any time; under any circumstances. It was usually my job to wake him when one of his events was coming up.*

*On this day, they had made the last call for the long jump, and I saw Bob in a lump over on the infield, so I went over and shook him awake.*

*On his first jump, I watched him go past 23 feet and started laughing. "What's funny?" he said. "That was a pretty good jump."*

*"It was a terrific jump," I said, "But you took off on the wrong foot." Bob looked at me, did this little thing with his*

*feet as if he were re-creating the jump and said: "Yeah, I guess I
did."*

  *A 23-foot jump on a lousy take-off!*

But sports were just a pastime in those days, not a business.
The rules for amateur participation were very strict, and the profes-
sionalism of most sports was still years away.  No one made a living
in sports like tennis, ladies' golf, or track and field until someone set
up a tour, found sponsors, and in some cases, changed the rules of
competition.

Baseball, of course, paid a living wage if you were good enough
and patient enough to rise through the minors and reach one of the
16 major league teams.  Boxing paid big purses, but only to a very
few.  The NFL was in its infancy, struggling to meet its payroll, and
the NBA hadn't even begun gestating yet.

Except for the very few superstars in each sport, most professional athletes had to take off-season jobs to make ends meet, and
even there, there was a pecking order.  Those with recognizable names
were able to capitalize on their fame by selling insurance or auto-
mobiles. Others, not so well-known, pumped gas or worked in fac-
tories or on farms. (This, of course, was all before television became
interested in sports.)

So, with no TV and only limited radio coverage, I got most of
my sports news from the newspaper (which carried primarily just
local sports) and the MovieTone news at the movies, which carried
highlights of national sports events such as big football games, the
World Series, and so on. It took me only about an hour a week to
keep current on who was winning and losing what.

My mother and father had already set my priorities, and the
number one was spelled E-D-U-C-A-T-I-O-N.  They made sure
my performance in the classroom took precedence over anything
else.  For example, I was a terrible speller.  I'm sure you've heard the
line: "He couldn't spell cat if you spotted him the c and the a."  I
wasn't quite that bad, but close.  We didn't know about dyslexia at
that time, and I don't think I was dyslexic anyway, but I guess it's
possible.

My mother made spelling fun, though.  She set up spelling
bees with my brothers and friends and gave an extra cupcake to the

winner. So, not only did *my* spelling improve but so did the whole neighborhood's.

I also feel that my high school English teacher, Miss Lois Thompson, had a great deal to do with my academic development, especially my improvement in spelling. She was constantly challenging me to do better. One day in class I referred to my encyclopedia and she said: "Can you spell encyclopedia, Robert?"

I couldn't.

"Can you spell dictionary?"

I did a little better but still missed by a couple of letters.

She could tell I was embarrassed and frustrated, and she took me aside: "Robert, we're going to have a word-of-the-day quiz from a list of five words I'll give you the day before. And you *will* spell that one word correctly each day." Then she used that phrase I had grown so accustomed to hearing: "You can do this, Robert."

Through these guiding forces, my parents, my teachers, friends and neighbors, I learned the discipline to at least try to overcome my weaknesses.

But since whatever notoriety I might have gained is from sports, not academic pursuits, I shall now take you back to the athletic field. Sim Innes and I were as tight as friends can be, but sometimes, even between friends so close, a problem can brew without one of the parties seeing it right away.

It was during the San Joaquin Valley CIF track and field finals in our junior year. The California Interscholastic Federation is the governing body for high school athletics in the state. Sim got off a huge discus throw, and I remember watching in awe as he let it go and thinking to myself: "Wow! They'll find that one in Bakersfield." It looked like it was launched, not thrown, and it carried 150 feet before it touched down. A CIF record for Sim!

We had a short celebration of his great toss, and then it was my turn in the box. There was no way I was going to let Sim's new record go unchallenged, so I put everything I had into my throw. It too took off and landed a 150 feet, 8 1/2 inches away. I had beaten Sim's state record, which he had held for all of about four minutes.

Since we had such a great relationship, I had no qualms about going over to him and giving him a little needle. But he surprised me. He and I had competed so often that it never occurred to me that he might be a little put out by my beating his great throw. He gave me a Queen Victoria-like "we are not amused" look and turned away.

At first, I didn't understand. Then when I realized it, I couldn't comprehend it. For God's sake, we had been through so much together. He beat me sometimes; other times I beat him. This was all just part of our cycle, I thought. As dense as I was, it took some of our other friends, Bob Hoegh in particular, to sit me down and explain how Sim was feeling. When I finally understood, I said to Bob: "What should I do? Sim's one of our best friends. Should I quit the discus?" I remember thinking that it still didn't seem like such a big deal to me, but if it was to Sim, I could live without it. Better to lose the discus than Sim.

Then a few days later, Bob told me that Sim was thinking about quitting school, which was *totally* ridiculous. If the discus meant so much to him, hell, he could be the discus man. I would just do other things.

### Jimmy Mathias (Bob's younger brother):

*I remember that incident. It affected Sim more than Robert realized at the time. Apparently, it had been building up in Sim that no matter how well he did, Robert always seemed to do better. It upset him very much; so much, in fact, that Sim announced he was giving up the discus. But it went even further. Later that week, there was talk around town that Sim was going to quit school, and, while he never said it was because he couldn't beat Robert, that's what everyone suspected.*

*I remember Robert was devastated. Sim used to be around our house as much as any of the family, but we went a couple of weeks without seeing him.*

*Then all of a sudden, Sim started coming around again as if nothing had ever happened. Robert had told some of his friends, knowing it would get back to Sim, that he was going to concentrate on long jumping and the hurdles, and that he was finished competing in the discus.*

*Most of Robert's other friends realized what he had done, and some of them even mentioned it to him, but Robert would never admit it.*

I remember people telling me what a noble thing I was doing by giving up the discus so Sim could dominate that event. How very naive they were. I wanted to keep Sim in school for his senior year. I *needed* to keep Sim in school for his senior year. He was the best offensive lineman in the San Joaquin Valley, and I was a half-back in a double wing offense. If Sim quit school, who the hell was going to keep me from getting massacred?

In our junior year, I had been strictly a blocking back, but Coach Virgil Jackson noticed I was always outrunning the ball carrier and promised to let me carry the ball as a senior. In those days, we went both ways, and I played one of the linebacker positions on defense.

One day, Sim crunched the quarterback and the ball popped up in the air; I grabbed it and took off down the field. I scored a touchdown with Sim trailing me looking over his shoulder to make sure no one was going to catch us from behind. We hugged in the end zone, and I knew then that everything was okay between Sim and me again.

### Virgil Jackson (Bob's high school coach):

*As a high school athlete, Robert showed the determination to excel. It was a pleasure to see him respond to coaching. With patience, he would repeat and practice until he had it right, while many athletes would come back for more coaching before they had progressed enough to warrant it.*

*In one football game, Mathias' combined running and passing yardage exceeded the total of the rest of the team.*

I was a busy guy that fall. I had a pretty good arm, so Coach Jackson put in a halfback pass series where I got to throw an occasional pass. I even got lucky and threw a couple of touchdowns.

Coach Jackson even found a use for my size-12 feet. He figured they might be good for more than running, so he taught me how to punt. So I not only was playing halfback on offense and linebacker on defense, but I was also punting.

By not playing both ways, I think today's offensive backs are missing out on a good experience and even some fun. If most running backs are like I was, they probably get a little tired of being hit all the time and not being able to hit back. When you play both ways, you get to dish it out a little as well as take it.

One particular situation stands out in my mind, not for anything spectacular I did, but for the outcome. In a game against East Bakersfield, I was getting creamed all day. On almost every play, I was getting the ball and the outside linebacker at the same time. This guy was all over me. But, I'm happy to say, on offense, he played halfback, and on a play late in the game, nobody blocked me, and I had my chance for revenge. I really laid into him for a 12-yard loss, knocked him cold and found out later  had even broken his wrist.

While he was on the ground, who should come out to tend to him but my father, who was our team's doctor and responsible for tending to the medical needs of both teams—and my brother Jimmy, who was the water boy.

### Jimmy Mathias:

*There's usually very little humor in a football injury, but this was an exception. I went out on the field with dad after Robert had cold-cocked this fellow. Dad was holding a smelling salts capsule under his nose while I was pressing cold cloths to his head and the back of his neck. When he came to, dad found that he had a broken wrist as well. So we helped him over to his sideline, and dad started to put a splint on the wrist. His coach came over to us and, in asking how his player was, addressed dad as Dr. Mathias. The player looked at Dad and said: "Dr. Mathias? Are you Bob Mathias' father?" Dad nodded and then introduced me as his other son. The fellow looked at me, and his eyes rolled back into his head. "What a family," he said. "One beats the daylights out of me and two others come over to fix me up. I think there are three too many Mathiases in my life."*

After the football season was over, what else could I do but go out for basketball. Good thing I didn't embarrass easily because my brother once told me I looked like a spastic windmill when I went for a rebound with my arms and legs going in all different directions.

### Eugene Mathias:

*Robert was a forward, but he was as fast and as shifty as any guard on the court and was second in scoring in the league as a junior. I honestly believe he would have been an All-American basketball player and encouraged him to stick with it, but that would hardly have compared with back-to-back gold medals in the Olympic decathlon. I'm glad he ignored my naive counsel.*

Time marched on, and once again it was spring, when a young man's fancy turns to thoughts of—track and field, of course! Even though I had publicly rebuffed the discus the year before, Sim decided I was being a jerk and challenged me to go back to throwing. After a long talk, Sim and I agreed that neither of us would hold back, but no matter what happened, we would always be friends, so we continued our rivalry. I was also becoming a pretty good hurdler and a fair sprinter. One afternoon, I won the hurdles, threw the discus 135 feet, won the shot-put, and, since our high jumper was injured, I had a try at that and won the event with a jump of 5'10".

# CHAPTER 2

# Remember the Phrase "Summer Job"?

**Good high school athletes** were a dime a dozen when we were kids, but none of us even approached the fame that some get today. I think the corporate subsidized summer leagues, especially in the inner cities, are wonderful. They give thousands of high school kids the opportunity to play through the summer, get good coaching and—not insignificantly—keep them off the streets. Obviously, there was no such thing when we were growing up, so we got summer jobs.

My first try at full-time summer employment was a disaster. The summer between my junior and senior year I got a job loading and hauling chemical fertilizer from a warehouse to a local airstrip for use by crop dusters. Not exactly a glamour job, but it paid an extravagant 50 cents an hour.

I was being entrusted to wrestle an ancient war surplus truck over country roads all by myself, and I was excited and full of pride. After all, now I was an adult. I was 16 and had just gotten my driver's license.

On my very first trip to the airstrip, I decided I would try double-clutching and promptly broke the shift handle off at the floor. So here I was, driving this truck full of fertilizer in second gear with no way to get it into high. What's more, if I stopped, the truck would stall, never to start again. So I was driving along these old country roads, the shift handle, useless as a duck's umbrella, lying across my lap.

Fortunately, Tulare wasn't exactly the traffic capital of the world, so I was able to chug through the back roads without having to shift. However, crossing the main road presented a problem. When I came to the intersection I had to cross to get to the airstrip, the light was red. Being the great thinker that I was, I whipped the truck into an orchard on the side of the road and watched over my shoulder until the light turned green, then I did a U-turn between a couple of fig trees, got back to the road and shot across the intersection. Of course, as soon as I stopped at the airstrip, the truck stalled.

My boss had to come pick me up and have the truck towed, and I worked the first six weeks of that summer to pay for repairs to that stupid behemoth of a truck.

But as all summers must, this too came to an end. And in September, I became the biggest of all possible big shots. I became —a senior!

Sim had developed over the summer and was enormous. He became an outstanding tackle at 6'5" and 245 pounds, and I topped out at 6'2" and 200. We had an excellent football season and got as far as the San Joaquin Valley playoffs before we lost to Roosevelt High School in Fresno, a much, much larger school. Pretty good for tiny Tulare Union.

Because of fantastic blocking like Sim's and others on the line, I was able to average over eight yards a carry and score 14 touchdowns. At the end of the season, Coach Jackson told me I had accumulated more total yardage than the sum of the teams we played that season: a total of 1,268 yards running and passing. If ever there was a tribute to an offensive line, it was in those numbers. It would have been great to have won the championship, but we gave a good accounting of ourselves that season.

We had a very good basketball season too, which was followed by my first love—track and field. Sim and I finished one-two in the discus at what was then called the West Coast Relays and later changed to the Fresno Relays. It was a major track meet then, as it is now. In fact, I was honored recently when the Fresno Relays were renamed the Bob Mathias Fresno Relays.

During that meet in May of 1948, I was able to get off a really good shot put and set the meet record with 54 feet. I won the high hurdles in 14.6 seconds, took second in the high jump, and won the discus with a throw of 141' 6 1/4".

Life was good. We had been undefeated in football until the championship game, and we had gone through our entire track and field season without a loss. If it hadn't been for a conversation with Coach Jackson in April, this would have been the end of my athletic career.

Coach had taken me aside back then and talked to me about something he thought would interest me. It was an event he called the decathlon.

I'll try to reconstruct a semblance of the conversation for you.

**Coach:** Robert, I think you should consider entering the decathlon at the Pasadena Games in June.
**Me:** June?
**Coach:** Well, you're in good condition.
**Me:** What's a decathlon?
**Coach:** It's 10 track and field events.
**Me:** Which 10?
**Coach:** We'll have to look that up, but I think you're probably doing four or five of them already.

Trusting fool that I was, I probably shrugged and said: "Okay, coach."

Why they were called the Pasadena Games I never did figure out, because they were held in Los Angeles at the Memorial Coliseum. Coach assured me that since I was already training for the

Fresno Relays, it would be just a matter of adding a few events to my training schedule.

Oh, little did I know . . .

Coach Jackson spent a day researching the events of the decathlon. He learned the 10 events comprised the 100-meter sprint, the long jump, shot put, high jump and the 400-meter race on the first day. Then, after having the whole night to rest up, the second day consisted of the high hurdles, discus throw, pole vault, javelin throw and a 1,500-meter race. "Hey Bob," I remember Bob Hoegh asking me one day while I was practicing. "What are you: an athlete or a track team?"

As you might imagine, this venture wasn't exactly problem-free. The problems started almost immediately when we found out that international track and field events are measured in meters, not yards, and none of us had any idea how long a meter was.

Another problem was the fact that, for safety concerns, there was no javelin event in California high school meets, nor was there a javelin in the immediate vicinity of Tulare, California.

Here's another. I'd been throwing a 12-pound shot in high school, and this event was for the big guys who threw 16-pounders. Problems three and four: Not only had I never thrown a 16-pound shot, we didn't even know where we could get one.

So we had an early deficit of one javelin and one 16-pound shot.

And yet another problem: Our high school hurdles were 39 inches high, but the meet called for the metric equivalent of 42" hurdles.

Coach Ernie Lambrecht, who had been a champion hurdler, assured me that if I didn't get some practice at 42", I'd hit every single hurdle. As perplexed as we were, the situation was even muddier after we thought about it. The CIF finals were still coming up while I was practicing for the decathlon, so I would have to practice hurdling at *two* heights: the CIF regulation 39" *and* the international height of 42". Very reassuring.

The final problem was one that didn't even occur to us that first day. It was the eighth event—the one they call the pole vault. The vault is arguably the most difficult event in track and field and calls for the most skill of all.  The problem was that I had never attempted to pole vault in my life.

Coach Jackson said: "You can do this, Robert.  You have more than a month to learn."

I shrugged and said: "Okay, coach" . . . again.

In trying to round up the equipment we needed and the information we lacked, Coach Jackson, Coach Lambrecht and I did what probably seemed like a version of "The Three Stooges Take Tulare." We were all over town.

We began solving the equipment problems when Coach Jackson borrowed a couple of javelins and a 16-pound shot from the track team at Cal State Fresno.  That left the difference between the 39" and 42" height a remaining hurdle (pun absolutely intended.) Coach Lambrecht fixed that ingeniously.

Fortunately, he was the shop teacher as well as coach, so he made slats that fit perfectly over each 39" hurdle, adding three inches of height.  It would be a simple matter to run a few heats at 42", then slip the blocks off and continue practicing at 39".  *A simple matter.*  That's what they told me.  *Everything* is a simple matter for the guy who doesn't have to do it.

One day, Coach Jackson came over to the track with a book and a huge smile.  "Look, Robert, this will solve a lot of our problems," he said, handing me the book.  "It's a book from Finland, and it's all about the decathlon."

This was exciting.  Now I finally had some worthwhile information on the event.  But my excitement didn't last long.  I took the book and started to go through it but stopped real quickly.

"It's in Finnish or something, Coach," I said.  "It's not in English."

"Of course it's in Finnish," Coach said.  "I told you it's from Finland."

"So how am I supposed to understand it?"

He gave me a disgusted look and took the book from me. "Here...," he said and started turning pages,  "...just look at the pictures, Robert. They show the events step by step."

"Oh," I said.  It seemed that I was saying "oh" an awful lot in those days.

Actually the book did help. It showed me how to hold the javelin and the approach for the pole vault, which I had never seen. But heck, I still had weeks to learn these events. No problem. *A simple matter.*

When the two coaches and I got down to L.A., we checked into the Coliseum and walked around on the field.

This was the field on which the 1932 Olympics had been held; the field on which USC and UCLA played their football games. I stopped and just stood in the middle of the field for a minute and looked around, probably with my mouth wide open. I was in total awe of where I was. There's a line in the Notre Dame fight song that goes: "Shake down the thunder cheering her name." Let me tell you, I was hearing some pretty loud thunder in that stadium, and I was covered with goose bumps.

I must digress for a moment to share a story. The (then) Los Angeles Rams had just moved from Cleveland and were playing and practicing in the Coliseum. Coming out of the locker room one day, I stopped at the water fountain, and, as I leaned over for a drink, I heard a voice behind me. Actually, it was more of a growl than a voice. "Hey kid," the growl said. "No drinkin'—it'll give ya cramps."

So I stayed thirsty. "Yes, sir, Mr. Legs," I thought to myself. How could I even think of taking a drink when Elroy "Crazy Legs" Hirsch had just told me not to?

And speaking of big names . . .

I just stood open-mouthed before the track meet started when guys like Floyd Simmons, Jerry Shipkey, and Al Lawrence introduced themselves. I know those names don't mean as much today, but back in 1948, these were *the* names. Simmons was the most famous name in track and field at the time and was using this meet as a tune-up for the National Championships, which he was heavily favored to win later in June. Jerry Shipkey was from UCLA; Al Lawrence was a USC legend, and any one of those three could have walked away with the meet.

But when Coach Jackson warned me not to be intimidated by these big names, it caught me by surprise. Intimidated? "Heck, I'm gonna beat these guys," I thought naively.

Call it pride or arrogance or whatever, but I've never been intimidated. Remember now, I was only 17 and was full of the hubris of youth.

Nervous? Yes.

Tense? Absolutely.

Butterflies? You bet.

But never intimidated.

I never in my life entered a track meet, a football game, an election, or any other effort without feeling that I could win. I'm not saying everyone should feel this way or even that it's right. It just happens to be the way I always felt before a competition.

So—here we were on what was arguably the most famous track in the world. The sun was doing its best to break through the Los Angeles smog. A bunch of the L.A. Rams dressed in shorts, T-shirts, and helmets were doing calisthenics in the middle of the field, and the head meet official used his megaphone to announce the last call for the 100 meters, the very first event in my very first decathlon.

I was taking a lot of kidding from the other competitors: "Hey kid, you have an advantage over us cuz your skin is so smooth." And: "Hey, kid, did you have your milk this morning?" Actually, I did, a couple of glasses. I still do, every day.

Anyway, I dug a little hole in the track for my push-off foot and took my mark as a huge flock of butterflies invaded my stomach. I was lined up next to Simmons, who was competing for the Los Angeles Athletic Club.

Then the gun went off and before I knew it, 11 $\frac{3}{10}$ of a second had gone by, and I was at the tape. I thought to myself: "Gee, there's no one in front of me. That's pretty neat. My first decathlon, and I'm in first place . . . . "

The next event was the long jump, which takes hours but seems to take forever by the time all the competitors take their three jumps. I was able to stay in first place by jumping 21' 4 $\frac{3}{4}$". Before the lunch break was the shot put. When I threw the shot 43' $\frac{1}{4}$", I was starting to get pretty impressed with myself. Here we are more than halfway through the first day, and the worst part is waiting around between events.

This decathlon stuff isn't so tough, I was beginning to think, and the next event, the high jump, was one of my best. No problem here. *A simple matter.*

Then I got my first lesson in what major competition was all about. The high jump, like the pole vault, goes on until there's only one competitor left. I dropped out after clearing only 5' 10", but Floyd Simmons kept pushing the bar higher and higher. I don't have a record of exactly what height he ended up clearing, but it was high enough to put him in first place. I wasn't used to getting beat very often, and, by having done so well in the 100, the long jump, and the shot put, I was probably getting a little cocky.

Simmons' whipping me in the high jump so easily made me a little nervous. I started thinking all kinds of thoughts. Had he been just toying with me earlier? After all, he'd been here many times before, and I was brand new. What did he know about me that I didn't know about him? I wished I knew what his records were in the events to come, but in those days, we didn't have that information, except for vagaries. For example, we might know a guy was good in the throwing events and bad in the speed events, but that was about it.

My biggest concern was: "Could I actually beat this guy?" In retrospect, having these doubts was good for me. I would go into the next event less confident but more determined.

The next event—the 400 meters—is the final event of the first day, and it's like a jailbreak. It's an all-out sprint for a quarter mile and is one of the most physically exhausting events in all of sports. The 100 meters, by comparison, is a piece of cake. You just run like hell for a 100 meters, and you're done. The mile? The mile is tough, but you go out fast on your first lap, then kind of just stay with the field for two laps and finish with a strong last lap.

In the 400 hundred, though, you're sprinting all out, as if you were running the 100, but four times the distance. I've seen world-class runners heave their guts after a tight 400, so why should anyone be surprised that the sadistic bastards who invented the decathlon in the first place should pick the 400 to end the first day?

Anyway, in my impetuous desire to get this day over with, I ran a 52.1 400, which put me back in first place with a point total of 3,689 to end the first day of competition.

I've been putting this off as long as I could, but I suppose the time has come to explain how the decathlon point system works. (If you want to take a little nap or maybe clean out the garage, I'll come get you when I'm through.)

Scoring was easy when I was competing, but there have been many changes in the point tables, primarily to keep the scores in relationship through the years, by compensating for the dramatic improvements in equipment, such as springier tracks, fiberglass vaulting poles, weighted javelins, and so on.

One of the most important improvements is one that no one ever mentions. It's those huge foam cushions the high jumpers and the pole vaulters fall into instead of landing in sawdust pits. Not only are they higher off the ground so that the drop is less, but you don't have to worry about landing on your feet. You can come down any which way you want and not get hurt. We had to finish up our vault and high jump so that we could land feet first in the sawdust, which by an odd coincidence was the same distance going down as it had been going up.

In an effort to be able to equate one era's points to another's, the International Amateur Athletic Federation has changed the scoring tables many times. From 1912 through 1962, scoring was based on Olympic records. For example, in 1912 the scoring awarded 1,000 points for the current Olympic record. That meant if the Olympic record for the long jump was eight meters and a guy jumped eight meters, he got 1,000 points. If he jumped seven meters, which was 87.5% of eight meters, he got 875 points. With me so far?

On later tables, from 1934 through 1962, scoring was done on a statistical basis in which the 100th, say, best mark in the individual events would be worth 1,000 points. For example, let's say the 100th best distance in the long jump is 7.80 meters. A guy jumping 7.80 meters will get 1,000 points. A guy who jumps seven meters will now get 897 points because seven is 89.7% of 7.80. This was still logical and made sense.

Today, I have no idea what they base the scoring tables on. Here's what my friend Frank Zarnowski has to say about the way decathlons are scored now:

**Frank Zarnowski:**

> *Unfortunately, the current IAAF tables have no statistical nor theoretical basis whatsoever. They were simply sketched, have no basis and are completely subjective. In 1984, when we saw the proposed new tables, no one—and I mean no one— thought they were worth a damn. I was surprised when the IAAF adopted them.*

Are you thoroughly confused? Don't worry about it. You'll never have to score a decathlon.

Okay—nap time is over. It's time to come back with me to Los Angeles, where the first day of the decathlon has just ended.

That night, after dinner with my mom and dad, I went to bed early and, using mom's relaxation method, was asleep within minutes. It's a good thing too. If I thought the first day of a decathlon was tough, the second day really was designed to separate the men from the boys.

I created problems for myself in the very first event, the 110-meter hurdles, by running only a 15.7. This put Floyd Simmons back in first place, but after having lost first place to him the day before, then regaining it in the 400, I didn't have the same doubts that had assailed me the previous day.

In the discus, it took my third, and final, attempt to finally get off a decent throw. But I finally got one off at 140 feet and was back in first place at the end of that event.

Now we were ready for the pole vault: The event I had been dreading. The vault is the hold-your-breath-and-pray-for-the-best part of the decathlon.

It is the event in which Dan O'Brien, odds-on favorite for the gold medal in 1992, no-heighted in the Olympic trials to eliminate him from that year's games in Barcelona. Dan eventually got his gold medal in Atlanta in 1996, but is a living example of how the vault has broken more than one heart.

Each vault must hurtle a 200-plus pound man over a bar, which is roughly twice his height. (Using today's magnificently flexible fiberglass poles, vaulters easily achieve *three* times their height and more.) Just standing in front of the bar and looking up at it is daunting.

As in all the field events, each competitor gets three attempts at each height, but in the vault, which goes on literally for hours, psychology plays a major role. If you clear a height on your first try, you're sitting pretty. You can figure to rest for sometimes as long as a half hour while the other competitors try to clear that height. If you miss on your first try, then you start to think about the second try. If you make it on your second try, you're still in good shape. But pity the poor guy who misses his first two tries. He *has* to make it on his third try, or he's gone! (See Dan O'Brien.) When you come down to your third try in the pole vault, it's like going for it on fourth and long in football.

After the first round, everyone who has cleared that height starts over again at the next height. Everyone who failed gets to rest up a good long time for the javelin. Each vault takes a little more out of your arms, your legs and your back, but you have to keep going until you miss a height on all three tries.

*The pole vault and the high jump are the only events in any sport in which eventual failure is guaranteed!*

If you're good, or lucky, or both, you'll be the last one standing at the end of the event. So here I was, after a couple of months of (hopefully) learning how to vault, missing my first two attempts at nine-and-a-half feet (a ridiculously low height by today's standards). I had been watching these other guys sail over the bar and desperately didn't want to see those dread letters, DNH (Did Not Height), after my name. I had cleared that height and more in practice, so I knew I could make it. I just had to convince my body. I knew I was doing something wrong with my feet, so I went over to another runway after my second miss and tried to work out the problem.

This was a lot better for me mentally than sitting around worrying about my third attempt.

When it was my turn for my third (and maybe last) try, I took off down the runway and felt the jolt in my arm and shoulders as I jammed the pole into the slot just right. Using my arms and legs, I threw myself into the air, went up, up, up—and cleared the bar by more than a foot. But—horror of horrors—I felt myself brush against the bar on my way down and my breath caught in my throat. I hit the sawdust pit—looked up and—that old bar was bouncing and shaking and shivering, but glory be, it was still up there, right where I wanted it.

I cleared a couple more heights and stayed in the competition until 11' 9", when I just couldn't go any further. However, the 729 points I got for the vault kept me in first place with only two more events to go.

The next event was the javelin throw. It wasn't part of CIF competition, so I had little experience in it, but I wasn't worried about it. I knew I had a good strong arm, so my throw of a 175 feet didn't surprise me.

By the time the javelin was over, it was almost 5 p.m. I was tired and hungry, and I just wanted to get out of L.A. and go home to Tulare, but there was the little matter of the 1500 meters, also known as the metric mile, to contend with.

This is another legacy of those descendants of the Marquis de Sade who gave us the decathlon. They said: "Let's create nine events over two days that'll completely exhaust the strongest and swiftest competitor. Then, for those who are left, we'll reward them with a mile run at the very end." Then they went off for a cup of wine, giggling and elbowing each other in the side.

By this time, I knew that I just needed a decent time in the 1500 to win the decathlon, and I was able to run a 4:59.2, which was worth 419 points, raising my overall total to 7,094 points—good enough for the win.

However, during the meet, I learned that Floyd Simmons wasn't at his peak because of injuries and sickness, so I thought of it as a bit of a tainted victory. For the record, the first five finishers after me were: Simmons in second place with 6,860 points; Jack Kaiser (San Diego State): 6,736; Ken Mitchell (San Diego State): 6,297; Ken

Beck (San Diego State): 6,121; Jerry Shipkey (UCLA): 5,894. Al Lawrence had dropped out because of injuries during the first day, along with a number of other competitors.

There were a lot of surprised people, and the question was asked more than once: "Who is this kid, Mathias?" I was beginning to get a little tired of this "kid" business, but I was going to hear a lot more of it over the next couple of months.

Whether Lawrence and Simmons were at their best or not, I had won the only decathlon I had ever entered, and it was a wonderful way to end my track career. Or so I thought—again.

# CHAPTER 3

# A Great Adventure

**Again, Coach Jackson had different plans.** A day or so after the meet, he and a man named Si Tyler, who was the head of the AAU in central California, showed up at the side door.

**Coach:** Robert, the Olympic tryouts are in two weeks in Bloomfield, New Jersey.

**Me:** Uh-huh. So?

**Coach:** Mr. Tyler here thinks you should go to the tryouts.

**Me:** (probably) Huh?

**Coach:** The Elks Club has agreed to pay your plane fare, and the AAU will take care of the costs of your hotel . . .

**Me** (interrupting rudely): Plane? I'd go on an airplane?

This was the most exciting prospect I'd ever had. I was going to fly!—to New Jersey yet. I knew that was near New York, which was all the way on the other side of the country. Wow! This would be my first time out of California. For once, I didn't think about placing or even competing. I was beside myself with excitement at the thought of a plane ride.

This time, I had almost two full weeks to practice, but this was big time: the Olympic trials! In addition to Simmons, Shipkey, and Lawrence, the legendary Irv "Moon" Mondschein, the '45, '46, and '47 National Decathlon Champion, would be competing as well.

The butterflies I had felt in L.A. were nothing compared to the way my stomach was jitterbugging as we lined up for the 100 meters in Bloomfield.

"The kid" didn't look like such a superstar during the first day. With Mondschein competing and Floyd Simmons healthy, I didn't finish better than second in any event and ended the first day in third place. I knew that third place would get me on the Olympic team, which was about as exciting a prospect as any 17-year-old could imagine in those days. But I was thinking, as I was walking off the field at the end of that day, that it would be great to be a team member, but wouldn't it be nice to *win* the trials?

Again, mom's lesson on how to relax came in handy. I slept that night as if I were dead and woke up ready to go. I learned later that Mondschein and Simmons were so nervous about the chance to go to the Olympics that they couldn't sleep.

I had 3,833 points going into the start of the second day, and Coach Jackson told me he thought 7,100 points would win it. I ran a 15.1 in the hurdles, which earned me 912 points and moved me up to second place. The discus, which was usually one of my better events, betrayed me, and I could only manage 138' 7". This got me another 788 points but didn't move me up in the standings.

So I was still in second place with the pole vault, the javelin, and the 1500 meters still to come. It had been humid, drizzly and overcast all day, but now the skies opened up, and the rain really came down. After about an hour, it let up to a slow drizzle, then eventually stopped. To try to dry things off, the officials poured gasoline all over the pole vault runway and lit it. The result was a spectacular blaze that had great entertainment value but didn't do much to dry the runway. The landing pit had become drenched and, as the water soaked in it got baked by the flames and took on the texture of concrete: very unpleasant to drop into from 11 feet in the air. The pole vault took even longer than usual with the rain delays and the attempts at flammable evaporation.

However, a couple of hours into the event, it dawned on me that most of the leaders had dropped out, and there I was still vaulting. I only reached 11' 6 ¼", but it was worth 696 points. I literally vaulted into first place.

My javelin throw of 157' 3" was pretty weak. In fact, it was almost 20 feet less than I did in the L.A. meet, but probably because of the weather, no one else got off a particularly good throw, and the 550 points held up to keep me in first.

When the gun went off for the 1500, I knew I had the meet in the bag. I already had 6,779 points, and if Coach Jackson's estimate of 7,100 points to win was even close to being accurate, I could have waltzed around the track four times and won. I ran a hair over 4:55 and ended up with 7,222 points.

I should point out that, unlike today, with electronic scoreboards and television statisticians keeping information flowing like an open tap, we had only a rough idea of where we stood in relation to the other competitors.

We relied heavily on word-of-mouth reports to tell us other competitors' times and distances in their heats. Our coaches would have notepads and pencils and do the arithmetic, converting times and distances to points on the scoring table.

I had heard tales of coaches figuring the numbers wrong and telling their athletes they only had to, say, vault 10 feet to take third place. The athlete would get up to 10 feet, then drop out to save his strength for the javelin and the 1500 and then learn much later that, in fact, he'd had to vault 10'8".

When the final standings and point totals were posted, it gave me the opportunity to tease Coach Jackson. "Gee, coach," I said. "When you figure points, you don't mess around." At the time he had told me 7,100 points would win the meet, he had no way of knowing that Irv Mondschein's second-place total would be 7,099!

Floyd Simmons scored 7,053 for third place and the final spot on the Olympic Decathlon team. Al Lawrence finished fourth with 6,640; Jim Roberson from Indiana University scored 6,744 for fifth and Billy Weaver, competing for Oklahoma University finished in sixth place with 6,488 points.

It would be Simmons, Mondschein and Mathias going to London. Everyone was surprised. I didn't admit it, but I kind of was too.

If I had been excited about flying to New Jersey, can you imagine how I felt about going to London? I learned that I enjoyed traveling then, and it's something I still enjoy today. Just wait 'til we get to the part where I get to tell you about the traveling I did for the State Department.

I went back home to continue training for a couple of weeks, then flew to New York, where the Olympic team was assembling. We were invited to a couple of lunches and dinners in our honor and spent some time in orientation sessions, where we got some books and literature on England and the history of the Olympic games. And we were given our uniforms. I stared at mine for a long time and kept imagining myself wearing it to represent my country in international competition.

We were to travel to England on the appropriately named SS America. As exciting as the trip was, I felt completely isolated because of my age.

I was on an adventure like no other in my life; the envy of any 17-year-old in the world. And I was lonely as hell.

# CHAPTER *4*

# Olympic Bound

**As we prepared to leave New York** for London, English and American forces, under the impression the war had ended three years ago, were beginning one of the most monumental ventures in history.

As a result of the Russian blockade of West Berlin in June of the year, millions of Berliners were in danger of starving. To send supplies in to West Berlin by truck would have risked a third world war, something neither President Harry Truman nor Prime Minister Clement Attlee were ready to do. So they came up with an alternative: the Berlin Airlift.

American and British planes and pilots, flying 'round the clock, landed an average of 12,000 tons of food, coal, clothing, and other supplies into Berlin's Tempelhof Airport every day!

This went on for over a year, until the Russians realized their blockade wasn't having the desired effect—to force the Allies to abandon West Berlin to the Russians. The Russians abandoned their blockade, and both east and west continued their tenuous peace. So, as we left for England, the world was technically, but not exactly, at peace.

The scene of our ship leaving the New York pier is one I'll never forget. A huge crowd was waving to us, and we threw streamers down to them. Then the ship backed out into the Hudson River, made a right turn and headed for the open sea. Dozens of us lined the railing, and as the Statue of Liberty slipped by, I began to realize that I, Bob Mathias, from Tulare California, was about to represent that statue and its flag and all they stood for in the first Olympic Games since 1936. God, what a feeling of awe came over me! I stared with tears in my eyes until it was out of sight. It was so magnificent.

I stood there, 6' 2", healthy and strong as Hercules and tried to picture myself as a refugee from Nazi Europe coming to America— or from the Irish potato famine—or from the Bolshevik Revolution.... What thoughts in their minds? What fears in their past? What hopes for the future? Could I possibly imagine the feelings of the millions of refugees traveling inbound and seeing that magnificent statue for the first time as the symbol of their new lives?

I could not. My life was too sweet; too full of warmth and love and dependable parents to know the horrors and devastation those immigrants to America had endured.

I can't say all of the team members looking out at that monument had the same thoughts as I, but I can tell you that it was very silent along the railing until Miss Liberty faded from view, and I know my eyes couldn't possibly have been the only ones not completely dry. Many of my teammates had recently fought the war to end wars for that statue, and I could only imagine the effect it was having on them.


These veterans, many in their 30s who had been cheated of the opportunity to compete during the war, accentuated my youth even further. There was a great deal of camaraderie among most of the athletes, but, of course, I was "the kid."

My roommates, or more correctly, cabin mates, were Moon Mondschein and Floyd Simmons, and they also referred to me as "the kid." Mondschein was, if anything a little too solicitous of me because of my age, and sometimes he would tell me to beat it, while he told a grown-up joke to Floyd. Where the hell did he think I'd been brought up, in a convent? Also, the kidding I was taking about not shaving was starting to get real old.

It was only natural that a few shipboard romances took place, but unfortunately, there were no girls young enough for me on board. Besides, most of the female athletes thought of me as—you guessed it—"*The Kid.*"

After suffering through days of rough seas and seasickness, we finally reached Southampton. We took a bus to an old Royal Air Force base in Uxbridge, which was to be our residence and practice site until the competition started. I began to get my land legs back and remember thinking the European competitors had a huge advantage over us since they only had to come across the channel, instead of spending five agonizing days on board a rolling ship.

At Uxbridge, I concentrated on those events that were still new to me: the javelin, and the pole vault. After the long layoff, I probably went at it too hard and developed nagging pains in my knees and elbow. A great way to start the Olympics.

World War II had led to the cancellation of two Olympic games, 1940 and 1944, and the '48 Olympics was filled with athletes who had lost the opportunity to compete in their prime. Fanny Blankers-Koen, a Dutch woman and mother, supposedly over the hill at 33, was the star of the women's track competition, winning the 80-meter hurdles, the 100 meters and 200 meters. She took home her fourth gold medal in the four-by-100 relay.

And there was a Czech named Emil Zatopek, who won the 10,000-meter run. Four years later, in the 1952 Olympics, Zatopek would turn in the most mind-boggling performance of those or any other Olympics. He would win and set new records in three events. Which events? Oh, nothing strenuous, just the 5,000 meters, the 10,000 meters, and the marathon. Did you get that? Let me translate: This guy won the three-mile race; the six-mile race; and the 26 mile race—and set records in all three!

We Americans had some real strength, too. Harrison Dillard took gold in the 100 meters, Mel Patton won the 200, and Mal

Whitfield the 800. Bill Porter won the 100-meter hurdles, Willie Steele the long jump, Guinn Smith the pole vault, and Wilbur Thompson won the shot put. The U.S. men also won the four-by-100 and four-by-400 meter relays, starting a long tradition of American dominance in those events.

The ride to the stadium was a somber one, going through parts of London that still showed rubble from the Germans' relentless bombing of the city. I remember at one point looking out the bus window at a neighborhood that still hadn't been rebuilt. I thought to myself: "My God, these buildings were actually *bombed*." My only frame of reference was to think: "Like the movies—but for real!"

And then, there I was, on August fifth, in London's Wembley Stadium, just six weeks out of high school and about to compete against the best athletes in the world.

# CHAPTER 5

# Just Call Me Bob

**I was so shaky in so many events** that I thought a couple of times, if I had a reasonably adequate IQ, I would have been back in Tulare hauling fertilizer. On the pole vault, in particular, I had gotten pretty good at getting up in the air, but I still wasn't quite sure how to get over the bar once I got up there. I had thrown the javelin only twice in competition and was having major problems with my footwork in practice.

My feelings are not easily hurt, but there was one time just before the competition began that I really got upset. I was just beginning to feel comfortable with all these great athletes when I heard that the Olympic decathlon coach, Ward Haylett of Kansas State University, told the press that I "showed a good deal of promise for 1952," but he didn't think I could repeat a win over Mondschein. He pointed out that during the trials, Moon had a sore arm and didn't do his best in the throwing events.

It was bad enough that I was lonesome and homesick and feeling like a kid among adults. I didn't need some insensitive coach implying to the press there wasn't much point in my being there.

To make matters worse, it made me wonder if maybe he was right. Maybe I had no business being there. But after awhile, I was able to put the comment aside. "The hell with you Mac," I thought. *"You just watch."*

There were more than three dozen of us when the decathlon started, but in the cold, unrelenting rain, they were dropping like flies. The grass on the infield was so wet and the ground under it so waterlogged, that on one of my shot put attempts the shot went so deep they had to dig it out—literally. On another throw, somebody's shot hit my marker, and they had to stop for a while to find it. Then I did an incredibly stupid thing.

I can plead that I was ignorant of the rules of international competition at the time, but I still should have known better. I got off a good throw and then stepped out of the box toward the front! Out of the corner of my eye I saw the official's red flag go up, and I jerked around toward him: "What? What did I do?"

International rules state that leaving the box from any location but the rear is a foul, and it voided my attempt. It was my best throw of the day, too, and it didn't count. It was a tough way to learn, but it taught me something. I swore to myself: "Come on, you stupid bastard, you can beat these guys if you stop doing dumb things."

Later in the event, some poor guy's shot went so deep into the mud that it was impossible to wedge it out, and, as far as I know, it's still there. Some day, an archeologist will dig it up and declare that a major battle had been fought on that site.

I was the center of a minor controversy in the discus event. I got off a good throw of nearly 45 meters (almost 146 feet). But later in that round, Irv Mondschein's discus slid through my marker, and, because of the rain and poor visibility, no one knew exactly where it had been. After much discussion, they arbitrarily replanted it at 44 meters even, but I know I had thrown it farther.

At the beginning of the second day, an Argentinian named Kistenmacher started playing mind games with me. He came up to me just before the hurdles event was to begin and told me that whatever I did he would do better, faster, longer, or higher. "*Don't give me that gamesmanship crap.*" I decided that even if I didn't win the decathlon, I would beat Kistenmacher—or I would burst into flame trying.

The conditions I just described notwithstanding, I have to say the track we competed on was a definite improvement over what I was used to. I had always run on a dirt or cinder track, which was exactly what it sounds like; an oval bed of ground-up concrete and cinders, not the bouncy, rubbery surface you have today. The cinders crunched when you ran on them, and little knife points crept into your shoes, sometimes bloodying your feet.

Speaking of feet, I've already told you about my size 12s, but guess what; they were still growing. Before we left Tulare, Dad decided I deserved a new pair of track shoes to take with me to London, so we went down to L.A., which was the nearest place to find size 12s. When the guy in the store measured me, he came up with 13.

This was getting a little embarrassing. To make matters worse, the salesman told me he hoped I wasn't planning to compete in anything serious. After all, he pointed out, size 13 feet weren't exactly ideal for running or jumping.

The track at Wembley was made of ground-up bricks taken from buildings that had been destroyed during the war. I didn't fully understand the hideous significance at the time, but thinking back years later, I pondered the stories those bricks could tell— about families destroyed by the war; about kids left without parents; parents who lost their kids; how could *we* ever imagine what it was like to wake up in the middle of the night to hear air raid sirens and the screech of Stukas dive-bombing your home?

When I did take time to think about it later, I wondered how many people had been killed or maimed in those buildings, and it made the Olympics pale drastically in significance. I'm glad I didn't have those thoughts at the time.

Anyway, as we approached the end of the second day, all of the competitors were equally miserable. We were cold and wet and exhausted. I didn't know about the others, but I was starved as well. I vaguely remembered having eaten something that day, but I had no idea what or when.

I have a mental picture of myself shivering in the cold rain, dog tired, soaked to the skin, staring at a pole vault bar as high as the Empire State Building. Then my mind drifted to Coach Jackson, and I couldn't help but laugh as I mimicked Stan Laurel: "This is some fine mess you've gotten me into, coach."

Looking back, I realize how lucky I was. Between my parents, Coach Jackson, Coach Lambrecht, some of my teachers and my friends, I was loaded with what would now be called a support group. I'm afraid a lot of that familial closeness is missing from kids' lives these days, and that's too bad. Kids need it, whether they're competing in athletics, in academics, or just plain living their lives.

Today, we're told how professional and well-run day care centers are, and that might be true, but they still create a situation where kids are being brought up by people who don't love them. Don't misunderstand what I'm saying. I'm not saying professional caregivers don't do a good job, nor am I saying they're not conscientious and competent. I'm saying they don't *love* the kids the way a mom and a dad love the kids. They can't possibly.

There is, in my opinion, no substitute for the security of mom being there when you get home from school. There was always something magic about coming home to cookies and milk.

As difficult as life might be for single moms, I believe they've made it even more difficult for their kids. It makes me very sad to see kids growing up in single-parent homes. They are not learning the same values we did earlier in the century.

Another thing: I often wonder if today's families really need two incomes to keep afloat. Oh, I know all about equal rights for women and glass ceilings. I respect women as much as anyone and more than most. My concern is for the kids and future generations being brought up in single-parent homes. And what the hell has happened to our principles? Today it seems totally acceptable to have a baby outside of marriage.

Sure, unmarried women have been having babies since the beginning of time, but at least it used to be socially and morally unacceptable. Our sense of propriety and morality seem to be in the toilet today. Today, babies born out of wedlock are so commonplace it happens on TV, and nobody seems to give a damn. Surely there are voices out there who believe this hurts the very fiber of our country! *I am not saying this from a religious or a moral point of view. I'm looking at it strictly as a qualitative lifestyle choice.*

Even in most two-parent homes, mom's not home anymore anyway, because we've become so acquisitive we're buying things before we can afford them, and mom has to go out and work. I know that credit has long been a way of life in America, but so has restraint. I remember my family doing without things until we could afford them. That's a concept that seems to be lost today.

*Easy for you to say*, you're thinking. *Your father was a doctor.* True, but we were far from rich. My father was the kind of doctor who accepted whatever a patient could afford to pay him. If he set your broken arm and you could pay him 25 dollars, great. If not, and you chose to pay him with a bushel of grapes from your vineyard, that was okay, too, and mom would make grape jam. My mother was educated, and she could have gone out and worked, but my parents felt it was more important that she be home for us kids when we needed her.

Okay. No more lecturing—at least for awhile. I have digressed. Let's get back to London, where it's now pitch dark....

The javelin throw, which is the next to last event, had catastrophe written all over it. Because of the combination of darkness, rain, and fog, the infield was like the bottom of a pot of week-old coffee.

One group of judges stood with flashlights trained on the foul line when we threw. But at the far end of the field—standing in total and complete darkness—were other judges waiting to measure the distance of each throw. We couldn't see them; they couldn't see us, and they certainly couldn't see the deadly pointed spears heading toward them. Shish-ke-judge was a very real possibility. Fortunately, we got through the event with no one getting skewered, and I got off a decent throw of 165 feet.

Coming into the last event, the 1,500 meters, AKA the metric mile, I was solidly in first place after more than 12 hours on the track. I thought of Coach Haylett's comment to the press. After finishing up the first day in third place, I had been in first place since the discus.

My closest competitor, the Frenchman, Ignace Heinrich, had run the 1,500 meters in an earlier heat, so I wouldn't be able to pace myself against him. On the other hand, it gave me an advantage. Already knowing his time and score, my brother Gene was able to figure out that if I ran the 1,500 in under six minutes, I would win the gold medal. Since I could easily run it in under *five* minutes, this seemed to be no problem, but I didn't realize how worn out my body was.

**Eugene Mathias:**

> *For two entire days, mom had been talking about the fact that Robert was just a boy, and he was competing against all these men. We kept laughing at her, but toward the end of the second day, it was apparent that the grueling two days had taken more of a toll on Robert than on the other, more mature competitors. Just before his heat in the 1,500-meter race was to start, I talked to him about Heinrich's time in an earlier heat, and I could tell he was having trouble concentrating on what I was saying. His face was drawn, and his shoulders were sagging, and he just appeared totally exhausted. I told him all he had to do for the gold medal was run the 1,500 in under six minutes, but I wasn't sure if I was getting through to him; that's how tired and disconnected he seemed to be.*

It was almost 11 p.m., and there was a lot of head scratching going on as the officials wondered how we were going to do this in the dark.

The stadium had been designed originally for daytime greyhound racing and had only some dim lights about waist high every 15 yards or so along the track. Well, what they did to brighten things up, those clever Brits, was to bring a bunch of cars into the stadium, aimed the headlights at the finish line, shot off a gun and said: "Have at it, lads."

**Eugene Mathias:**

*It was like a surreal slide-show watching the runners go past a light on the track, fade back into darkness, then materialize at another light. Because of the rain and fog, when they got more than 30 or so yards away, they disappeared entirely. Before I could see them I could hear them squishing because there was no one in the stands.*

*Robert knew what he had to do to beat out Heinrich for the gold medal, but wearing leather shoes on a saturated track can be daunting. He had only that one pair, and, in addition to being waterlogged, they had filled up with little clumps of brick dust. They must have weighed at least five pounds each. To make matters worse, there were big puddles all over the track, and each time a runner stepped in one, it broke his stride.*

I tried to stick close to Erik Anderson from Sweden because I knew he was a good miler. I figured if I could stay within striking distance of him, six minutes would be no problem. But as the race wore on, more and more space opened up between us, until I couldn't even see him any more. I was so tired and probably dehydrated that each time my foot landed, I felt knifelike pains shoot up my legs. At one point during the third lap, the thought even entered my mind: "*What the hell do I need this for?*" I was almost obsessed with how tired and wet and miserable I was, and I think I kind of fell into a trance and almost gave up. I had no idea how close to Anderson I was, and for a little while, I just didn't care.

But then I heard the bell for the last lap, and it kind of made me realize where I was and what was at stake. "*I've come this far,*" I thought. "*No way I'm gonna quit now.*" I knew I just had to go all out with everything I had for as long as I could. If I collapsed, so be it. I would come in under six minutes, or they'd scrape me from the track. Eugene had stationed himself at one of the turns and had been calling out my splits each time I went by, but I guess I was so tired I had trouble understanding what the numbers meant.

### Eugene Mathias:

*I was at one of the turns giving Bob his lap times, but he was so tired I could tell the numbers weren't making any sense to him. On his third lap, I thought it was all over. It seemed to be forever until I saw him, and I even started thinking maybe he had quit somewhere on the other side of the track. Up to then he had been on schedule to easily beat the six-minute mark, but now, when he finally came into view, he was shuffling more than running. His head was down, and his hands were at his sides, and he looked as though he was about to pull up and call it a day. But as he came to the turn he heard us yelling, plus there were some fellow Californians there; some students from Pepperdine University were shouting, "Come on Tulare . . . come on Tulare." He seemed to regain some sense of what was at stake and began digging into that reserve strength he's always had. Apparently, he kept it up for a full lap because the next time I saw him was at the finish line, where he came in at almost a sprint in an amazing time of 5:11.*

It's not quite true, what Eugene says, that there was no one in the stands. We didn't get quite the crowd they do today, but I bet there were almost 100 people there that night. My mother and father and brothers were there. And I know there was a reporter from the *New York Times* there, because he asked me afterwards if I spelled my name with one or two t's. My only thought at the time was that I would never—NEVER—put myself through anything like this again. I was more tired than I had ever been in my life.

The elation wouldn't come until the next day when I stood on the award stand.

**_Track and Field News Magazine_ (coverage of the 1948 Olympic Decathlon):**

*The story of the 1948 Olympic decathlon will go down in history as one of the wonder stories of all time.*

*It is the story of Robert Bruce Mathias, a 17-year-old man from Tulare, California. It is the story of how he defeated the greatest all-round athletes in the world despite the weirdest and most heartbreaking conditions with which any athlete ever had to contend.*

*It seemed all the fates were against Bob, and, in spite of his 6' 1 1/2" and his 195 (sic) pounds, he was regarded as too young to stand the strain.*

*The rain and the treacherous takeoff of Wembley Stadium were as bad for the others as they were for Bob, but he lost two feet in the shot put by an obscure Olympic rule which required him to step out of the rear of the circle. He came back strongly in the high jump and the 400 meters to finish the first day's competition in third place.*

*(At the end of the first day) Lieutenant Carlos Enrique Kistenmacher of Argentina was leading with 3897 points, 49 more than Bob's total. He told Bob: "Whatever you do in each event, I'll do better."*

*But the next day, Bob started out at 10:30 a.m. with a 15.7 clocking in high hurdles. He passed the confident Kistenmacher, but Simmons took the lead with a 15.2 pace, leaving Bob (still) in third place.*

*Another mishap occurred in the discus, when Mondschein's throw knocked over Bob's marker, and the officials had to spend 20 minutes finding it and, according to one eagle-eyed reporter, set Bob back 18 inches. Even so, he won the event and took the lead.*

*In the pole vault, he had to wait for six hours while other groups finished, and when he vaulted, it was too dark to see the slot for the pole. But Bob, one of the greatest competitors of any age, vaulted as high as his closest competitor had done in the daylight and retained his lead.*

*Now it was so dark the javelin line had to be illuminated by flashlight. Bob was tired, and the javelin is an erratic event at best, but Bob's great pitching arm hurled the spear to the better-than-expected distance of 165'1".*

*He had clinched the championship. All that remained to beat (Ignace) Heinrich's final total of 6974 was to drag his weary body around 1,500 meters in 5:49.1. There, in the darkness of the torch-lighted stadium, he put on a sprint that gained him a time of 5:11.*

*Then, 12 hours after he had started the day's events, he plodded barefooted across the turf to embrace his parents. Wearily, he said:*

*"No more decathlons, dad, ever again. I never worked so hard for anything in my life."*

There's a story which might be true, but I think it's apocryphal. At least, I never remember it. A reporter asked me how I was going to celebrate my victory and supposedly I said: "Start shaving, I guess." Even then, I *had* to be thinking of a better way to celebrate an Olympic gold medal than *that.*

It's a shame that so few people can ever know the feeling of standing on the top of a pedestal while your country's flag is raised. There is no feeling like it in the world, and tears were streaming down my face as the "Star-Spangled Banner" was played. And I'll tell you, anyone whose eyes remain dry in that situation is only marginally human. Today, I watch the Olympics from the stands, and I still get that feeling when an American stands there.

One difference between today's Olympic winners and me is that I had absolutely no idea what I had done. It had been 12 years since Jesse Owens had humbled Adolf Hitler during the 1936 Games. I was only five years old then and not exactly tuned in to international competition. By the time 1948 rolled around, I had no memory of past Olympics, and there I was, by the standard King Olaf of Sweden had applied to Jim Thorpe: The World's Greatest Athlete. (And to which Thorpe had replied: "Thanks, King.")

As you can imagine, there were congratulatory messages from all over, from friends and relatives; many from people I had never heard of.  Among all the notes and telegrams, there were two that I cherish to this day.  The first is for obvious reasons:

*By winning the Olympic decathlon championship you have demonstrated abundantly that the glory of America is its youth.  In the name of the nation to which you have brought such outstanding distinction I extend hearty congratulations.  All your fellow Americans are proud of you.*

*Harry S. Truman*

Another telegram was one I received after I arrived home.  I thought then and I still think now, that it epitomized sportsmanship as we knew it:

*Welcome home.  Congratulations and best wishes to the world's greatest all-around athlete and our greatest opponent. Best of luck in the future.*

*The student  body of Porterville High School*

Porterville was our arch-rival and we had been through some ask-no-quarter, give-no-quarter knock-down, drag-out battles with them on the athletic field.  Reading that telegram meant as much to me as any accolades I had received anywhere, from anyone.

Someone mentioned to me that I was the youngest decathlon gold medalist ever.  It didn't mean a great deal to me at the time, but now, given the rigors of training and the level of competition these days, I'm relatively certain no one younger than 17 will ever win the event.  And I'm *really* sure no one will ever win the Olympics after having competed in only two prior decathlons.

Today, I look back over the past 50 years and wonder how we got to the point of amateur athletes being paid million-dollar training subsidies by shoe companies; about our Olympic basketball team being made up of NBA players; about shoe companies deciding how we dress for the awards ceremony. I've thought to myself more than once: "What the hell ever happened to the Olympics?"

I wonder, will Michael Jordan look back in 50 years and say: "What the hell ever happened to basketball?"

Will Joe Montana look back and say . . . "What the . . . " well, you know what I mean.

I must say, I wasn't thinking these thoughts at the age of 17. These are thoughts that have come upon me since the onset of what has become the professionalization of amateur sports.

All I was thinking at the end of the '48 Olympics was how soon I could get back to Tulare. I was just tired and homesick and anxious to see my friends.

Perhaps I shouldn't have been so anxious, though. There was no TV to speak of in those days, so MovieTone News did a feature story on my win. It was showing in the theaters about the time we got home, and one night I went to the movies with Bob Hoegh, Sim, and some of my other friends, and they ragged me unmercifully when that segment came on the newsreel.

So—international celebrity? Right. To these guys I was: "Hey, Bob."

And I loved it.

# CHAPTER 6

# Welcome Home

**When my family and I got home,** we were greeted by a huge and unexpected welcome. I asked my mother what the fuss was, and she smiled at me.

"This is for you, Robert."

"No, seriously," I asked her. "What's going on?"

I really thought they were kidding. I had won in track meets before, and it had never been a big deal. The high school band was playing, the mayor shook my hand, my friends were all there, and, to my horror, I learned that I was expected to make a speech. A speech? I would rather have been a javelin catcher!

After listening to a lot of other speeches telling what a wonderful fellow I was, I finally got up on that stand in the middle of the town I had grown up in, in front of hundreds of people I had known all my life, looked around at these warm, friendly faces and— wanted to throw up.

I managed to croak, "Thanks," and went to sit down. There were a couple of polite but expectant smiles, and the mayor blocked my way. I waved again and smiled and expanded my speech.

"Thanks a lot," I said, but there was still expectation in the air. So I took a deep breath and started talking. I have no idea what I said, and I'm sure it wasn't particularly memorable, because nobody ever said: "Gee, Bob, that was some terrific speech you made." Since then, I've made many more speeches—some on the floor of the House of Representatives—but none ever meant as much to me as that first one.

My next stop was scheduled to be Stanford University, but I was forced into a detour. I had gotten a D in English in my senior year, so I had to spend a year at prep school to make up for it before I could be admitted to Stanford. Even though there were good prep schools in California, my family chose Kiskiminetas Prep in Pennsylvania, so that I could get the flavor of another part of the country. As it happened, my good friend Bob Hoegh attended *Kiski* with me.

After a year at Kiski, I was admitted to Stanford, and when I got there, it wasn't easy trying to balance a schedule that included football, track and classes.

And studying.

And research.

And library time.

I was on the track team at Stanford for all four years, but I only played football for my last two years. I was in a pre-med curriculum and was also doing a lot of traveling related to my Olympic victory so the demands on my time just didn't permit me to play football my first two years.

I also had to make a trip to New York that year to receive an award that means more to me now than it did when I received it. The Sullivan Award is awarded each year to the outstanding amateur athlete in the country. I questioned whether or not I deserved it since there were so many great athletes at the time, but they selected me, and who was I to argue?

Each year, when I note the current recipient, I kind of shake my head and think: "Wow, am I in good company . . . " Here are just a few of the Sullivan Award recipients: Glenn Cunningham, 1933; Felix "Doc" Blanchard, 1945; Dr. Sammy Lee, 1953; Harrison

Dillard, 1955; my good friend and the first female recipient of the award, Pat McCormick, 1956; Rafer Johnson, 1960; Wilma Rudolph, 1961; Jim Ryun, 1966; Frank Shorter, 1972; Bill Walton, 1973; Bruce Jenner, 1976; Carl Lewis, 1981; Edwin Moses, 1983; Jackie Joyner-Kersee, 1986; Janet Evans, 1989; Mike Powell, 1991; Bonnie Blair, 1992; Dan Jansen, 1994; Michael Johnson, 1996; Peyton Manning, 1997.

Quite a line up!

When I look back, I can see that the differences between today's athletes and those of my time are staggering.

The most obvious difference is that the athletes of today are faster and bigger and just plain better than we were.

They are the product of superior training regimens, better diets, better equipment, sports medicine's ability to recover more quickly from injuries, more knowledgeable individual coaching, and the development of newer, more efficient techniques.

For example, in the high jump, we did something called the roll, or sometimes, the western roll, which was basically a run, a dive at the bar, then a scissors-kick and a twist of the body so you went over sideways as opposed to head first. Today's Fosbury Flop (named for its creator, Dick Fosbury) lets the jumper approach the bar in such a way that he has more spring and leverage and can use both legs to propel him upward, then propel the body over the bar backwards, so he can more easily clear it with his legs and with less chance for stray clothing or body parts to knock the bar off.

Better equipment plays a major role too, especially the composition tracks and the foam pillows that let a jumper or vaulter come down on his back or shoulders.

Then there's the fiberglass pole used in vaulting. Pssst—here's a sneak peek at some sports history. I was the first guy to vault with a fiberglass pole. In 1948, we vaulted with steel or bamboo poles, but I was able to switch to fiberglass for the 1952 Olympics.

Here's how it came about:

Coach Jackson had an off-season job at a company that made fishing rods and masts for boats out of fiberglass, and one day he asked his boss if he could experiment with a vaulting pole. He worked on it for months before he even told me about it. One day, he came over to the house with three poles and asked me to try them. I tried one and noted immediately that it was much lighter than a steel pole and much stronger than bamboo. It still didn't have any of the amazing flexibility you see in today's poles, but that would come later—as an unintended consequence.

I worked with these poles for months, until one day, during practice, I planted one in the approach slot, and it cracked, practically disintegrating. It actually came apart in my hands the way a dried flower might if you rubbed it. It turned out that the glue used to bond the materials had dried, causing the pole to crumble. No problem, though. Coach could make more.

Years later they began using a new glue—one that wouldn't dry out. Not only did it not dry, but it gave the pole that extreme flexibility it has today that practically whips the vaulter over the bar. So—I didn't have the flexible one, but I did have fiberglass, and I was the only one to compete in the '52 games using a fiberglass pole.

I mentioned diet earlier. The food we eat today is so different from what we thought was going to make us strong and healthy a generation ago, that it's a miracle any of us survived. We were encouraged to eat red meat, the more the better, and I knew some guys who could pass for cannibals. They gave us fried eggs, bacon and sausage for breakfast; hard-boiled eggs and hamburgers for lunch, and steak for dinner. Hungry after dinner? Here, have another burger or a few hard-boiled eggs and a milkshake. Who knew about cholesterol? About the only constant is that, even then, we knew smoking was no good for us.

And liquids—oh, the difference in attitude toward liquids!

The common belief, as Crazy Legs Hirsch had pointed out to me that day in the Coliseum tunnel, was that if we drank anything during a heavy practice we would get cramps, so we were denied liquids. We were allowed to take water in our mouth but were told to spit it out, not swallow. And we believed them! One of my most vivid memories is from an August day when it was over a 100° in the shade. We were on the football field at Stanford doing wind sprints, and my mouth was full of cotton and peanut butter. I actually tried to chew on some grass for whatever moisture I could get from it.

Today's athletes should fall on their knees to honor whomever theorized that liquids are an essential accompaniment to physical exertion.

Playing football at Stanford was actually fun. We earned our letters and wore them proudly around campus. I'm not sure that has the same meaning any more. I get the feeling that today's college athlete is as much a part of the student body as a bank robber is part of the Federal Reserve.

I went to Stanford because it was my school of choice and because my brother Eugene was there, not because of what they offered me.

In fact, they offered me nothing.

Can you imagine? Here I was an Olympic gold medal winner, on record as *The World's Greatest Athlete,* a high school football star, and I couldn't even get a scholarship. They told me we had too much money. Where *was* all that money, I wondered.

I suppose today I would be known by that bizarre term, a "walk-on."

I didn't qualify for a scholarship at Stanford, but they did help me get a job. I was the campus rep for a clothing store in Palo Alto. I didn't get paid, but I did get my clothing at a discount. Unfortunately, we seldom wore much other than Levis and T-shirts and a sweater on the occasional cool evening, but it was nice to know that if I ever *had to* get dressed up, I could do so at a discount.

I have to say the Stanford years were wonderful years, and I truly believe it's a shame today's athletes aren't more a part of the student body than they are. I don't fault them; I fault the system that has taken them away from campus life and set them up in their own private world.

For example, I remember reading an article about Joe Paterno in which the writer was impressed by the high percentage of Paterno's players at Penn State who graduate.

Think about that.

*The high rate of football players who graduate.*

What does that statement tell you?

The fact that Penn State's high graduation rate is even worth mentioning tells me there's something terribly wrong. It tells me that a great many athletes are no longer going to college to learn, but rather just to hone their talents, then, hopefully, on to the pros. They're like gladiators brought into the arena for the entertainment of the Roman Emperor. If they got hurt, well, too bad, but they did their job well.

Too many of today's athletes are *at* the college, but they are not *of* the college.


The following is addressed to some university official who cares.

I have an unorthodox idea; a challenge, really, for you to do something for these kids—your gladiators.

By accepting them with SAT scores and high school grades below your school's minimum acceptance level, you've already acknowledged the fact that they are not intellectually capable of pursuing your standard curricula. You've accepted the fact that they will never go on to become doctors or physicists or cabinet members, but maybe you could teach them to become *cabinet makers.* Or plumbers. Or something!

Why not institute a curriculum that adds vocational studies to prepare these scholarship athletes to be useful citizens if they don't make it to the pros? Restaurant dishrooms are full of 6'8" *black* kids who were *sure bets* to make it in the NBA!

Oh sure, I can hear it now. *"What?! We're dedicated to higher learning! We can't lower our academic standards to the vocational level."* Listen, you've already lowered your standards by admitting these kids as mercenaries. Now do something for them. Set up a special course of study that will teach them a trade so they can make a living if they never make it to the NFL or the NBA—and statistics show overwhelmingly that most of them won't.

You have to recognize and acknowledge the fact that your scholarship athletes are cut from a different cloth than your other students. Put in courses that will prepare them to get along in the world in other respects. If you don't want to teach them vocations, at least teach them how to interview for a job, how to dress, how to make a good impression, how to look an employer in the eye, how to stand, how to walk. Teach them some basic lifestyle skills.

Teach them that turning on the automatic sprinklers on the athletic field doesn't prepare them for a damn thing!

Give them self-marketing courses, so when they don't make it to the pros at least they don't come away from your school empty.

Also, for those who do have a legitimate shot at the pros, have courses available to them *from the business department*, not from their coaches, on how to interview, select and deal with an agent, how to analyze investment opportunities . . . and similar skills.

In some cases, these kids' bodies and motor skills have been developed and nurtured for 14 or 15 years. Surely some college can afford to put in a year or two on their intellects.


I know this will sound like heresy coming from a Pac-10 alum, but I have to say I think the Ivy league schools have it pretty much together. I'm not talking about their academic excellence—that's a given—but rather about their approach to athletics. There was a time when Yale, Columbia and Penn (that's the University of Pennsylvania, not Penn State) ruled college football.

Then, through the late '40s and '50s, they de-emphasized their sports programs when they felt the growing competitiveness of big-time college sports was detracting from the real reason kids go to college. Today's Ivy League athletes are *full-time students who happen to play on a school team.* They're not on athletic scholarship nor have any academic standards been lowered or waived to permit them entrance. They had to pass the same entry exams to get in as non-athletes and have to maintain the same grades in the same courses as non-athletes to stay in school; and even higher grades to remain eligible.

The Ivies offer their own version of college sports. They play each other, plus some schools with the same philosophy, like Williams, Amherst, Bucknell and others. No Ivy League school will ever be a national champion again. But Penn's basketball team did make it to the Final Four in 1979 only to lose to a Michigan State team with a young fellow nicknamed "Magic" something.

And in 1995, Princeton beat mighty UCLA in the first round of the NCAAs, so miracles do happen.

But here's my point: Do the Ivies feel they are left out of college sports? Are you kidding? Sure Stanford vs. Cal and Ohio State vs. Michigan are big games, but so is Harvard vs. Yale. You'll see as much passion on the field as at any game. And the Princeton vs. Penn basketball rivalry is as fierce as any in college.

# CHAPTER 7

# The Home Field Advantage

**Sorry. I didn't mean to lecture.** Let's get back to the task at hand. Before we fast forward to 1952 and the Helsinki Olympics, I'd like to tell you a little about my domestic track career.

My next decathlon competition was the AAU Championships held the summer of 1949 on June 28 and 29. Since the only recent gold medal in the Olympic decathlon resided in Tulare, the AAU graciously decided to hold the championships there. What could possibly be more advantageous to me than to have the national championships held on the track I had grown up on!

When Marcus Aurelius said that fame was ephemeral, he wasn't talking about a 17-year-old Olympic gold medal winner living in a town the size of Tulare. I took the *home-field advantage* to heart and scored my highest total to that time: 7,550 points. I ran 11.3 in the 100 meters (if nothing else, I was consistent in that event), which started me out in fifth place. I was still in fifth place after the long jump but moved into second by the end of the first day. When we started the second day, I ran the hurdles in 15 flat, which just squeezed me into first place. Then I ended the suspense by tossing the discus almost 152 feet. By the time we got to the javelin, I knew I had the meet in the bag.

There were 17 finishers, the top six being Irv Mondschein in second with 7,044 points; Bill Albans, third; Bill Terwilliger, fourth; Floyd Simmons, fifth; and Ken Beck of San Diego State, sixth.

A month later, Mondschein, Albans and I found ourselves in Oslo competing against the Scandinavian countries. Again, I put together enough good scores to win the meet by a couple of hundred points. Orn Clausen of Iceland edged out Irv Mondschein by just six points for second place. Two Swedes, Per Eriksson and Kjell Tannander came in fourth and fifth, and the other American, Bill Albans, placed sixth.

By the time we got home from Oslo, it was just about time to start school. Mom and Dad loaded the family Ford with just about everything Eugene and I owned, stuffed us into the back seat and headed north to Palo Alto.

I was looking forward to representing Stanford on the track even though there would be no decathlons during the NCAA meets.

In a way, it was nice being able to pick my events, but, believe it or not, I missed the rigor of the two days of the decathlon. There was something about slugging it out event by event with the same guys, knowing we were all in the same ordeal together. There's also something about decathletes that's indefinable. Maybe it's a misery-loves-company kind of thing, but I enjoyed it then, and I enjoy watching it today. However, the NCAA competition was marvelous, and it kept me sharp and in shape.

### Frank Zarnowski:

*The most amazing thing about Bob Mathias's career in the decathlon is that he never lost. I mean that literally.* Bob Mathias never lost a decathlon! *He competed for five years in two Olympics, five national championships, the world championships in between Olympic years, college meets, exhibitions...* he never lost a meet! *And to make it even more incredible, he kept breaking his own world record right up to the '52 Games when he not only destroyed his own record, but won the event by more than 600 points!*

*Now, what does that mean?*

*It means the man was invincible. Daley Thompson of Great Britain is the only other guy in the world who ever won back-to-back Olympic decathlons. Daley won in 1980 in Moscow (when the Americans boycotted) and in Los Angeles in 1984 (when the Soviets returned the boycott favor). The boycotts really did not taint his victories. In those days, no one was going to beat him. But even Daley, a two-time gold medalist, lost a few decathlons in his career.*

*BUT BOB MATHIAS NEVER LOST!*

*The capital letters are deserved.*

*Another point that should be made: Bob was so young when he won all those decathlons. He was the youngest man in virtually every field. When he won in London, he was only 17, as everyone knows. But when he won in 1952 in Helsinki, he was still only 21, one of the youngest in the field. Twenty-three of the 27 Olympic decathletes in 1952 were older. Bob retired before most decathletes get going!*

# CHAPTER 8

# A Letter From Mom

**I have a good recollection** of the 1950 National Championships, partly because they were held again in Tulare, but mostly because of a letter my mother wrote to my brother Jimmy when he was away at Kiski Prep. Jimmy kept the letter and made a copy for me. It's a rather long and chatty letter, and in some parts a little disjointed, but I'm including it in this book because it gives an excellent sense of the flavor of our bucolic small-town life mixed with the hustle and brutishness of national and world competition.

It shows that mom was pretty savvy about the sport and the competitors. It also shows how different things are today. A modern-day decathlete might read this letter and accuse me of making it up. *...Come on Mathias—the governor came to your house after the meet? Who d'you think you're kiddin?* Someone recently read this letter and commented: "This sounds like Mayberry versus the world!"

## Letter from Lillian Mathias to son Jimmy, July 9, 1950:

Thursday night
July 9, 1950

Dear Jimmie:

Here's the Decathlon Story:

Thursday was hot at 8 a.m. and by 11 it was around 100 degrees. Don Winton and his wife came out to the house with Terry Fitzhugh, the 15 year old boy from Pasadena. He is about 5'7" and 150 lbs. A nice kid but sure didn't even look 15 years old. He was just more than impressed with the trophies and Robert and everything. Then Brayton Norton came out. He is a prince of a kid. Not good looking but a quiet sincere boy that Robert liked immediately. Then several others came by . . . Floyd Simmons, Tom Bowman from Florida that had the cutest Southern accent, and even Bill Albans was here. Robert stayed up in his room and sweltered and played records and rested. I fed him a small steak, some lettuce and sugar, and some orange juice about 3 p.m. All of Daddy's folks were here so we had supper and watermelon in the back yard. Jack Wieirhauser and Ray came over along with Virgil Jackson, and we all went over at about 6. There were 30 of u . . . Almyra came down from Berkeley with a friend of here, Uncle Paul from Fresno.

They had a wonderful ceremony with a torch. Bill Naugle ran in with a small torch and lit the big one just as in the Olympic games. Then they marched with flags representing the states the boys were from. Each boy..contestant...was introduced and stood on a platform and took a bow. Robert was the last one but did he get a big hand. He looked the best too, because some of them had on dirty grey sweat suits . . . and Robert wore his red Satin Tulare suit..clean, bright and shiny.

It was so hot the boys didn't have to warm up much. Robert didn't have to run with Albans . . . and got in the second heat of the first flight. You remember last year Albans got first and Robert and Mondshien tied for second when Moon was 6 feet back of Robert? This year the officials tried out their watches on the first flight and Robert got a fair deal.

The broad jump was good. Robert had power and determination but poor form so they said. Ray and Jackson said he didn't have a single good jump out of the three . . . fouled on his second try . . . his first was the best. Albans began to make wise cracks and even though he jumped 24'6", he tried to better it and wasted a lot of energy. Simmons did his best that night too. He had never jumped 23 before but he did and fouled. He was happy though in knowing that he could do it.

Albans began telling the boys that Tulare was full of a bunch of yokels, that Robert was just a dirty little A-hole, and that even if he didn't do anything but stick his nose in cow manure, the SOB's of Tulare would root for him anyway, when they were seeing the best athlete in the Nation perform, namely Albans. Robert was tense and tight . . . we knew he was disturbed . . . then when he put the shot, Ray jumped up and went out to the fence to talk to him. He took a few practice shadow throws and Jack W. went out along with Eugene. He got out a 47'6" on his second shot and the third was a few inches less. Eugene came back to sit with us and he was fit to be laid out . . . he said Robert had reverted back to his high school method of putting and that he had forgotten everything Ray, Jack or Dean had ever shown him. It was just power and not form that got it out. We all felt sick because he had been hitting close to 50 every day in practice.

Then he went to the high jump . . . tried and cleared 5 feet, 5'3", 5'6", and when they got to 5'10" he was stuck. Missed twice. Albans started raving and told him he was "grandstanding." He went over and started to throw sawdust in the faces of a bunch of Robert's fraternity brothers who were working on the field. They had encouraged Robert and told him he could make it. Albans used the worst language that was ever heard in Tulare, I guess. They were afraid that he would go crazy if they said anything to him but he even told the officials that he knew they were crooked and that if he won they would try to disqualify him so Tulare's little A hole could win. Robert was so nervous he kept snapping his fingers . . . finally took a long run, chopped a few little steps and cleared the bar. The crowd went wild, Albans got madder, and I just sat and cried. They raised it 3 inches and Robert cleared on the first time to get 6' 3/4" inches. They raised it another three inches and Robert went out but Bill made it. Then he tried for 6'4" and failed. He took 30 minutes for that last height . . . he yelled to the crowd, he cursed Robert and swore the town was against him. It got quiet and he yelled "I'll bet whoever said that is afraid to come out of the stands" and not a soul had said a word. Finally after running up to the bar a half dozen times he jumped and failed. He missed twice again and we all thought he was going to throw all the sawdust out of the pit.

Then they ran the 400 meter. Robert was completely pooped. Daddy honestly looked scared because he didn't know whether he would make it or not. It was still hot . . . the sweat was pouring off of us all. I rushed home and cooked Robert a steak while he took a shower and then he went to bed. Eugene, Jackson, Ray, and Jack W. got around the table and did they figure! Albans last year ran a 55.4 400 meter . . . this year he was so mad he was crazy and he ran a slow first half then came in to run a tremendous 49.5. He told them he had spent 4 solid months on the pole-vault and could do anything Robert could do in that. He said he could out run Robert in the 1500 . . . and no one knew how to figure him because he had actually run the 400 like he said he would. We knew Robert had him in the Javelin and discuss . . . Albans could take the hurdles and the vault and 1500 were a toss up. I didn't go to sleep until 4 a.m. and I guess the officials didn't either. Next morning Harold Berliner came out to the house and said according to the rule book Albans should be disqualified, but since he was ahead, that he would declare to the end of time that he would have broken the world record, had Tulare not disqualified him so their Bob could win. So they trusted in the Lord to see that Robert came thru without anymore had luck . . . and let Albans stay in . . . to prove to him that he was not the world's greatest athlete but the all time poor sport.

Friday was terrible. Dozens of people came to the house . . . I kept things quiet . . . Fed Robert and Norton at 3 p.m. He was tense and nervous and I know a little scared . . . I was on the verge of tears. Brayton was sick with the heat so he went up stairs and stripped and slept on your bed. By 5 o'clock the temperature was 114. Dean and Jackson and Jack came over and ate hamburgers with us and we all felt like something was going to explode. Just before we left the house Robert went into our bedroom and laid down across the bed. Jack and Ray went in and I closed the door. I guess they said the right thing because they came out and Robert motioned for us to come in. He gave me the old good luck sign and told me he was ready to break the record and for me not to worry. I felt better because he seemed to be in better spirits. We all went over at 6 p.m. again. Governor Warren landed at the airport at 6:15 and they told him the hurdles were to be run at 6:30. The State Troopers put the sirens wide open and they got in the stadium at 6:25. Mrs. Warren and two daughters, Nina and Dorothy were with him, and believe me, they are just as sweet and gracious and good as he is. They sat with us and with Robert 93 points behind, we saw Albans run a beautiful 14.1 hurdle race. Robert was right at his heels as they figured he would be. I felt good because I had dreamed that he hit every hurdle for a week . . . and he ran a beautiful form. Ray just sat and grinned and rubbed his hands.

They used only one discus ring there on the track that you were working out on with Robert. The track was so hard that it was difficult to get a good throw . . . they couldn't get a footing . . . seemed to slip while in the spin. Robert got his good one first . . . only 146'5" the others a few inches less. He was terribly disappointed because he had planned on at least 160. Ray and Jack and Eugene had disappeared . . . and I'll tell you about that.

Before the hurdles, Eugene and Ray went to check the vaulting pole and discus for Robert. The pole had been hanging in the store room with 20 others the day before and Tulsa Phillips said the building had been under guard. But Robert's pole was gone. They checked and Si remembered that someone had used a pole on a float in the parade the day before, and maybe that was it. They got a cop and went to find Jack Sherman . . . 85 miles per with the siren wide open. Jack was gone so they came back to the field and by that time someone said that the float that had used the pole had been dismantled at Richmond's Garage. So Craig Tyler, Eugene and the cop started out again . . . 90 miles per . . . got down there and couldn't get in. The cop covered his hand and broke the window . . . they boosted Eugene and Craig in and they tore the place apart, still no pole. Finally Eugene saw a door that was locked and he asked the cop what to do, he said, "Bust it in." E. got off about two yards and "busted" the door broke in half . . . and there in the office was R's pole. E. poked it through the window to the cop, who put it on the side of the car and turned on the siren. They drove in with the pole about ten minutes before he was ready for his turn. Eugene was wet with sweat . . . his pants didn't have a dry thread. He looked worn and haggard and triumphant. He was breathing like he had run a marathon. Craig was just as bad. Jackson was smoking like a steam engine . . . shaking like a leaf and speechless. Then he was so scared the pole would break that he came over here and sat in our back yard. He said he prayed that the pole wouldn't break. He knew he would never make another one if it did . . . he was sunk, through, finished. Then he heard the crowd roar. Quiet. Then a roar. Quiet. Then it sounded as if the town had gone crazy. Quiet . . . more silence . . . then the lid blew off over there and he could stand it no longer. He ran back to be told that Robert had just cleared 13 feet 3/4 inches for a new Stanford Frosh record as well as a new personal record and 898 points. Gee, I wish you could have seen that guy. He was so happy I thought he was going to sink thru the stands. We all began to feel wonderful again . . . but first let me tell you about the pole vault deal.

Robert sat out until the bar was about 10'6"..cleared it and 10'9" and 11. Then he sat out until the bar was raised to 11'6". Everyone thought he had been disqualified and made such a fuss, I asked Daddy and he said he was saving his energy. Boy if he had missed the next height he would have been out . . . but good. But he didn't. He made 12'3", 12'6", all with one try. Then Albans and he were all that were left of that flight. Albans tried for 11'9" and missed. Robert cleared by a foot, so Bill took two more tries, cleared both but knocked the bar off with his hand. Did you by any chance hear him swear back there? He GD'd everyone and everything, and they go a picture of him throwing sawdust . . . look in Advance Reg . . . then he picked up his sweat suit, beautiful white and pale blue satin, and started beating the ground with it. He started walking until he got to the hedge at the north end of the field and there he laid down and kicked. While they were raising the bar to 12'9" for Robert. Rob walked down there to Bill and told him to get back up there and keep plugging . . . there were still two more events to go. Robert left him and they raised the bar, he had his first miss. On the second try he cleared. He grinned and people went crazy because he was ahead of Bill in points on that. He thought he was thru but Jack W. was sitting there and he casually said... "If they raise it another 3 inches..it will be 13'3/4", and if you clear that you will have the Stanford Frosh record back." Robert turned to the officials and said, "Raise it." Mrs. Schultz was sitting there and saw the bar go up and she thought they were making him do it . . . she started yelling "You can't do that to Rob. You can't." Mrs. Warren grabbed a hold of the Governors shirt and held for dear life. They asked for quiet so the competitor could concentrate on that height (Robert was the only one left) and I saw him wetting his lips and rubbing his fingers together, then he walked slowly back, stood there about three minutes just staring at that bar, we were all breathless  . . . then he started down the runway. You will never know how I felt and I am sure others were just in the same boat. He cleared it the first time by about four inches. 898 points. Mrs. Warren had the governor's shirt tail almost out . . . she put her arm around me and we both cried. People just couldn't believe it. They announced over the loud speaker that Ray Dean had just said, "That is all for tonight, Bob." So they walked down to the javelin runway. Gov. Warren sure tickled Daddy. When Albans missed the third time he said real loud," Aww..he missed" then turned to Daddy and said "Thank God."

Ray told Robert to get a good one out his first try and then forget the other two so he could be resting for the 1500. Simmons, Albans then Robert threw . . . the first one sailed out 182'4", and the crowd nearly stomped the bleachers down because the others were way back . . . Albans 134'. His other two throws were around 179' . . . not bad either. Norton was the only one who was near him and he had one 175.

They rested about 30 minutes then the first flight or top 6 started out. Daddy couldn't stand it so he went over to the finish line with Eugene. Jimmie . . . Jack W. came up and sat by me and the Gov. and he showed us that Robert had the record broken if, IF, he could run the 1500 in 5 min. 35 seconds. I knew he was tired, we figured he had run 7 or 8 100 yard dashes besides the energy of flipping himself over that bar and it was still over 100 degrees in temperature. He missed the bar only once in going over ten times . . . good. So he we pacing himself to run a 5 minute 1500. He did pretty good the first three laps but the last 200 he sure looked bad. People stood up and yelled and cried and begged him to keep on going. Nobody around us had a stop watch . . . we all knew he was going to miss it by seconds . . . he didn't sprint a step, just kept plugging slower and slower. Daddy and Eugene caught him as he fell thru that string. Then they announced that he had made it in 50.5.1. or 29.9 seconds to spare. London was never like that. All tarnation turned loose. Some people swear the asphalt pavement started to roll up like a rug and Hanford called to see what had happened. Daddy and Eugene walked him a while, he could hardly stand, then he realized the record was his and he sure had a big grin. When I get copies of some of the pictures I will send them back to show you.

Then the people crowded around, Gov. Warren signed autographs, so did I, and Robert and Ray and Jack. I finally got away and came home to get Robert something to eat. The Warrens, Dorothy and Nina, about 10 Phi Gams, the Bakers, the Glicks, the Harris', PH and MJ, grandmother Gates, Almyra and her friend, the Okla city bunch, the three coaches, and I don't know how many others came over. I had made 10 gallons of punch and had ham, cheese, potatoes and corn chips, 3 big cakes, two peach cobblers, a tubful of carrot, celery, olives etc. so we spread it out and passed the paper plates. Stayed out there and hashed it over until nearly 2 a.m. Then people started leaving and by the time we all settled down it was 3 a.m. Then Daddy and Eugene and I went up to Robert's room and we talked another half hour.

There was just one thing we regretted about the whole thing, you were not with us. Next year, if Robert competes, and I think he will, you are to be right out there on the field with him to see that things go right . . . what with the missing vaulting pole and Albans, it was more than Eugene could take care of. I have another idea too. If Terwilliger is as good in track as I think he is, and you are as good an athlete as I think you are, then I might be the only mother in the world to see two of her sons competing in a National Decathlon at the same time. There were four high school kids competing and you could have beat all of them and probably nosed out Wilkinson of Drake and Price of Wheaton college. We will see what you can do and keep it a secret until next June.

Uncle Marion sure had a time, and Eugene. Barney Franklin asked E. if the governor actually came over to the house. Eugene said, "sure, and he used the toilet, come on over and see, we haven't flushed it yet." That held Barney. Then Patricia took the two Warren girls to the bathroom . . . Robert had just finished his shower and I told Robert afterward that he should have picked up his clothes, that Nina got her foot caught in his jock strap as she came out. That held Robert for awhile. We all had fun and felt so happy that so many people were happy too. I guess it was worth all the worry and work.

Eugene lost 5 or 6 pounds and he didn't see the hurdles or the discuss. Bobby Abercrombie said if Eu. had seen the discus he would have lost more than that for he had figured him for 160'. Robert knew the pole was gone, but they didn't tell him that they hadn't found it, you probably could have beat him if he had known the truth. Albans was another factor that made things so hectic.They kept asking Robert if he bothered him and Robert said no, but no one can stand and take what he did and not be affected. Another thing ws that World Record idea. He figured he had to improve 40 points in each event to make over 400 points to put him over, and points are sure hard to make when you get up that high. The tension of knowing everyone wanted him to make them must have been terrific . . . it was for me.

Well Jimmie, I think I have told you all about it. The Elks gave a beautiful big 2 foot trophy and he got his third gold medal. I have hundreds of clippings to put in his book and more keep coming in. He got a bunch of telegrams and yours is the only one he wants to put in his book to save. He is still autographing and getting fan mail by the dozen.

Any questions? I'll answer any that I have forgotten if you ask. Dean Pryor, Art Kurtz, Floyd Simmons, Big Jim R., dozens of others asked about you. Zamzow said they told fabulous tales about the Mathias BOYS at Ripon College, in Wisconsin, and he was terribly disappointed in not seeing you. He was sure a nice kid, reminded me of Dick Drilling except he had more personality. We called him "Blacky" and his pal was "Smokey." We were crazy about Tommy Bowman from Florida too, he talked with a real drawl.

Must close and get this "report" off to you. Hope it answers some of things you want to know.

Love and kisses to my Kiski Kid,

Mother

Later that summer, I got to go to Europe again to compete in the Swiss Championships. This was the first time I was in first place from start to finish (I even won the 100 meters). A Swiss, Armin Scheurer, finished second; Davorin Margelja from Yugoslavia was third; Oto Rebula, also from Yugoslavia, fourth; an Italian, Lorenzo Vecchiutti, was fifth; and another Swiss, Hermann Notter, finished sixth.

I was enjoying not only the international competition but meeting and getting to know the boys from other countries as well. It was a gradual process, but I was beginning to form plans for my future that would permit me to continue traveling and meeting people from other lands.

Once in a while, I'd feel I was getting into some bad habits with one event or another. When that happened, I'd try to compete in that event to get the added practice. Vaulting and the javelin, in particular kept getting me out of synch, so I'd spend time on those two events whenever I could.

The academic year 1950-51 was pretty uneventful for me. There were no decathlons of any note, and I was able to concentrate on my studies and compete again on the Stanford track team.

*David Edwards (javelin thrower, UC-Berkeley, competed against Bob in college):*

*The scene was Edwards Field on the UC-Berkeley Campus. The occasion was a dual track meet between Cal and Stanford. Excitement had been building with the anticipation that Bob Mathias would be competing in several events.*

*As one of the less-than-star quality freshman trackmen at Cal, I was particularly excited by the opportunity to meet Bob at the javelin run, since that was my event also. Bob had set a world record at the 1948 Olympics, and everyone was eager to see him in action. I recall the special qualities about Bob that impressed me. He walked with the balance and poise of one with a well-disciplined body. There was no swagger of arrogance or grandstanding around the infield. Rather, there was a calm assurance that, having tested his skills in the crucible of Olympic competition, Bob knew what he was capable of achieving and was prepared to do his best in each event.*

*While I had a brief conversation with Bob, I did not distinguish myself with a memorable or competitive throw. However, the memory of competing at the same track meet with Bob Mathias is one I have not forgotten.*

In my junior year, I switched my major from premed to education, with an eye toward becoming a teacher and someday perhaps a coach. Coach Jackson had such a positive influence on me, and it was he whom I hoped some day to emulate.

An education major obviously was less demanding than medicine—*anything* would be less demanding than medicine—so I felt I could comfortably go out for football in my junior year.

As strong a presence as track was in my life, my strongest memories of college athletics are not from track but rather football. And my most vivid memory of football involves a person much better known than I will ever be.

It was during the 1951 season, and we were playing USC for the PAC-10 Championship, the winner to go to the Rose Bowl on January 1, 1952. We'd been ahead by seven points, but USC had just scored to even things up. When they kicked off to us, I took the kickoff on our four-yard line and bobbled it. It fell to the ground but fortunately popped straight back up into my hands. Incidentally, someday some smart coach will put that maneuver in his playbook, because when it happens, the kicking team always lets down a little, assuming the return isn't going anywhere.

Anyway, with the whole USC team bent on doing me harm, I finally got control of the ball and headed up the center of the field. I remember a couple of really good blocks as I cut to the right sideline, and then all of a sudden there was no one between me and the goal line except the USC kicker. He approached me at an angle, and I slowed myself down ever so slightly so that just as he was about to hit me, I would have a tiny burst of speed I could use to get past him. I ended up scoring a 96-yard touchdown; we won the game and went on to play in the Rose Bowl.

For many years, while watching Monday Night Football, I would think of that play and that USC kicker who missed the Rose Bowl by one tackle. He was one of the best football players of the day, an All-American halfback named Frank Gifford.

Today, when I see Frank, I like to tease him about that little episode. He invariably gives me a blank stare and says something like: "I'm afraid I don't remember. Did we ever play against each other?"

January 1, 1952, we played Illinois in the Rose Bowl, which was an indescribable thrill. If someone could find a way to harness the pent-up energy and excitement an athlete feels during a big game like that, and dole it out over a lifetime, I don't believe anyone would ever show signs of aging.

And it was quite a game—the first half anyway. Our quarterback, Gary Kerkorian, got a concussion that we didn't know about until the third quarter, which is when he started throwing passes to guys in the wrong colored jerseys. One went for a TD; the other all the way to our five-yard line. When he asked someone in the huddle who we were playing, we figured it was time to call a time-out and get him out of there.

Coach put in Bobby Garrett. Bobby was a fine quarterback, but he had a minor impairment. He stuttered. It's okay if you stutter in the middle of the line or at the ends. It's okay if you stutter at center. It's even okay if you're a halfback or a fullback, because the rule is that nobody talks in the huddle but the quarterback. When a quarterback stutters, it's serious and funny at the same time. Since my place in the huddle was next to Bobby, it was my job to jam him in the side when he stuttered and couldn't get the play called. He was okay most of the time, but once in a while, he'd get hung up on a consonant, and I'd have to defibrillate him with an elbow to get him back on track.

We'd had a terrific first half and were ahead 7-6, but apparently we forgot a football game has two halves. Illinois scored 34 points in the second half, and they whipped us 40-7.

# CHAPTER *9*

---

# Sim and I—
# The Gold Rush is On

**Okay, now it's time to get serious about Helsinki.** That summer, the AAU Decathlon Championships also acted as the Olympic trials, and *again* they were held in Tulare. Apparently, the AAU officials were treated so well by the townspeople that they kept wanting to come back. That was fine with me. I loved mom's cooking!

The name of a new decathlete began appearing on the sports pages, and I was anxious to compete against Milt Campbell. Unfortunately for Milt, I broke the world record again at the trials with 7,825 points, but he came in second with 7,055, and Floyd Simmons placed third, beating out Bill Albans for the final Olympic slot. My mom didn't appreciate Bill's attitude toward all things Tularean during the 1950 Championship meet, so she was pleased that Milt, Floyd, and I would be going to Finland and not Bill.

By the time the '52 Games came around, I had broken the world record for the decathlon a couple of times, and, unlike 1948, I was a heavy favorite to win. This created a different kind of pressure from what I had felt as a wide-eyed innocent in London.

Back in 1948, I was so excited about just going to London, the idea of competing in the Olympics was almost secondary. When I was "the kid", little if anything was expected of me. It would be great if I did well, but if I didn't, *well, he's only 17, what do you expect?*

In 1952, however, a lot of things had happened to change the world scene, and I didn't feel like an innocent abroad any longer. There was something that was euphemistically being referred to as a police action on an Asian peninsula called Korea, and Senator Joseph McCarthy was finding Communists behind every tree and lamppost in Washington. The Rosenbergs had been executed for giving atom bomb secrets to the Russians. President Truman had approved the development of a hydrogen bomb. The Egyptians were rioting against the British; the Germans and French were at crisis point (again) over the Saar Basin, and thousands of people a month were pouring into West Berlin from the East.

The Cold War was heating up, and most of the world was thinking: *World War III, here we come.* The national mood regarding the Olympics was us vs. them.

I like to think Milt, Floyd, and I were thinking in more idealistic terms, but I know, for myself at least . . . as much as I wanted to beat Floyd and Milt, there were two other guys I wanted to beat more. Their names were Vladimir Volkov and Sergei Kuznyetsov.

As I said, I was no longer *Die Wunderkind.* This time out, I was the heavy favorite to win the gold medal, which held a certain responsibility I had never before felt. Milt Campbell was also highly regarded as was the 1948 silver medal winner, Ignace Heinrich, from France. And of course, Floyd Simmons, the 1948 bronze medalist could never be counted out.

I felt the pressure from the opening gun and ran a great (for me) 100 meters. Unfortunately, someone ran it faster, and I was already in second place—not a good beginning.

My long jump was a so-so 20' 10-3/4", but its 779 points were enough to move me into first place. I stayed in the lead throughout the rest of the meet and was still there to win my second Olympic gold medal after the 1,500 meter run at the end of the second day.

I recall a couple of interviews after the competition: Two reporters confided in me that there had never been any doubt in their minds that I would win. "We knew you wouldn't let your country down, Bob." Oh yeah? I wish I'd had that kind of confidence.

The '52 Games were so entirely different for me than the '48 Games had been, it was almost as if I were two different people. In 1948, I actually didn't know what I was doing. I was strictly raw talent—strength, speed and agility—*Civius, Altius, Fortius* as the Olympic slogan says: Swifter, higher, stronger. I was like a windup toy. Put me on the track and see me run.

In 1952, on the other hand, I was the favorite and had to listen to how impossible it would be for anyone to beat me. Yet I was reading about the power and expertise of the Soviet training machine and how secretive they were about their methods and their athletes. There was an Estonian named Heino Lipp who, a reporter from his country bragged, would have whipped me in 1948.

But he wasn't there in 1948, and he wasn't there in 1952, either, so the point is moot. The race is not only to the swiftest, it's to the guy who shows up.

Now, in 1952, there was another supposed Russian superstar named Vladimir Volkov and an East German named Josep Hipp. I had no idea what these guys were capable of, and, now that I think back, I guess it didn't much matter. I just knew I wanted to win.

I was never so determined about anything in my life. Call it patriotism, jingoism or whatever, I *would* bring another gold medal home to the USA and Tulare!

The reporters could write whatever they wanted about how invincible I was. I knew better. I knew that any guy out on that track could beat me, and I was the guy they were all gunning for. I also knew about injuries and quirks of fate. No one—*no one*—is ever a sure thing in any event, especially one that lasts two days.

There's a funny thing about decathlons. It only takes one bad event to make you a footnote. You can lead the field for event after event then fall in the hurdles, no height in the vault or the high jump, stumble in the 400, foul out in the long jump—you get the point. It's two days of gearing yourself up physically and psychologically for the next event, then the next, then the next.

Often we'll read a newspaper account of how an athlete easily *won* an event. Don't believe it. Those *easily won* events can just as easily be lost.

### Fulvio Regli (Olympic reporter)

*From the standpoint of competition, there was little or nothing in it, though, since top placings never happened to hang in the balance. The eagerly awaited duel (of) Campbell-Heinrich behind the invincible Mr. Decathlon did not materialize because the Frenchman sustained an injury to his left foot during the high jump event....*

*The meet was no win or lose problem for Bob Mathias—the only thing to decide was whether or not he would beat his recent Tulare record.... (As it turned out, Glenn) Morris' Olympic record (of 1936) was pulverized.*

I have to say that winning another gold medal was a huge thrill, but it was made even sweeter when I was able to appear on the awards stand flanked by my American teammates: Milt Campbell with a silver medal and Floyd Simmons with the bronze. When the band began to play the "Star-Spangled Banner," I snuck a look at both Milt and Floyd and found out they were sneaking looks at me, and, yes, we all were embarrassed behind our smiles because we'd been caught crying.

Here's some trivia for you. Actually, it doesn't even qualify as trivia. It's *minutiae.* I'm told that I'm the only guy who ever played in a Rose Bowl game and won an Olympic gold medal in the same year.

A day or so after I won the decathlon—*Glory Be!* My cup ran to overflowing as I watched my very dear friend Sim Innes take the gold in the discus. I had hoped against hope that he would win the event, but the competition was *so* stiff and *so* unrelenting that I knew Sim would have to work his heart out to win it, but he did, and my joy knew no bounds.

I remember sitting in the fading Finnish sun, wiping my eyes during Sim's award ceremony, and thinking what a year this was. It started out in the Rose Bowl, and here I was now in Helsinki with a gold medal in my pocket and another one about to be dropped around Sim's neck! As Ira Gershwin wrote: "Who could ask for anything more?"

Sim knew I was there in the stands, and somehow—in that huge crowd—his eyes found mine. From afar, our eyes spoke in a language only lifelong friends can understand. We knew there was no other town in the world the size of Tulare with two gold medals coming home.

Here's a footnote for you. In 1952, Tulare won more track and field Olympic gold medals than Germany, Great Britain, all of Asia, all of Africa and all the nations of South America—combined!


The newspapers all told us that we Americans had "won" the Olympics with 43 gold medals for the U.S. and only 22 for the Soviet Union. The Soviet press, on the other hand, put a different spin on it. They assigned point values to each medal (i.e., five for gold, three for silver, one for bronze) and according to *their* system of scoring, *they had won the Olympics.*

Nobody wins the Olympics for heaven's sake! The Olympics then—and the Olympics now—shouldn't be about which *country* wins the most medals. It should be about individual effort and the opportunity to compete against the world's best. Nation-by-nation scorecards are anathema to the whole idea of the Olympics!

# CHAPTER *10*

# Touring the Continent —1952 Style

**Once the closing ceremonies were over,** reluctant good-byes were said, and the competitors headed off to their own parts of the world and resumed their lives. Except for some, including Lillian Mathias' second born and his friend Sim.

The AAU included Sim and me, along with some other Olympians, as part of a series of goodwill tours of Europe.

My group stayed in Helsinki for awhile, then went on to Germany with stops in Cologne, Dortmund, Sollinger, and Berlin. After that, we went to Zurich, Switzerland; Stockholm and Goteborg, Sweden; and Edinburg, Scotland, returning home in late August. Decades before "Where's Waldo?" ever appeared in the comic strips, my folks were playing "Where's Robert?"

At the end of the tours, Sim and I flew into San Francisco, and, to our surprise, the city had a huge parade for us. Then we drove down to Tulare, where they had another parade and more welcoming ceremonies.

The European tour was the first of many I would make abroad for the AAU and then for the State Department as their Goodwill Ambassador. I enjoyed meeting the people of these different countries and found their customs extremely interesting. Comparisons between life in the U.S. and life in these other nations were inevitable.

It was these early trips that spawned my interest in people of other countries, their customs, their histories, and their governments and eventually led to my decision to run for the U.S. Congress.

After the summer's travels, life began returning to normal; at least, normal for me. I didn't realize at the time how my life had changed in the four years since that rainy night at Wembley Stadium in 1948.

In September 1952, I returned to Stanford to get my degree, and, like college seniors from the beginning of time, I thought to myself: "Now what?"

In case you've been thinking of me as an athletic machine, I'd like to dispel that thought. I did have a life outside the locker room, and today I have three fantastic daughters, Romel, Meagan and Marissa, and a fantastic son, Reiner, to prove it.

One day, I was sitting in class and looked across the room. I saw a face I had seen before, but this time I saw it in a different way. The face belonged to Melba Wiser from Modesto, a small town in California's central valley, not unlike Tulare, except larger. "*Hmmmm*," I thought. "*You could do a lot worse, Mathias.*" Soon after that, Melba and I started dating, and as so often happened in those days, dating led to—plans.

And the plans were that soon after graduation there would be a Mr. and Mrs. Bob Mathias. Making money was no longer a nicety. It was to become a necessity.

When I graduated from Stanford in June 1953, I looked around for ways to make a living. Surely there was something for a two-time Olympic gold medalist to do, even though I knew I couldn't make a living competing at track.

Just as a side thought, I wonder if today's track zillionaires realize there was a time when all they could have earned was a gold medal and a wreath?

In December '52, I had been asked by the AAU to help put on track clinics in Acapulco and Mexico City and was glad to do so, but the subject of compensation never even came up. But I also had to make a living.

Actually, I did have a couple of employment options, one of which was professional football.

I had been drafted by the Washington Redskins, but I wasn't sure that was how I wanted to spend my post-college years. A good fullback in 1952 could make—*maybe*—$10,000 to $12,000 a year. I figured I could do better than that pursuing something less likely to leave me with a permanent limp. And there was another factor. Tulare High's nickname was the *Redskins*; Stanford, at that time was known as the *Indians*; and now the Washington *Redskins* wanted me to play for them. Enough was enough already with Indian nicknames.

You could say that I was decades ahead of the rest of the country in sensitivity awareness, but that really wasn't the case. Nor is it now. Which leads me to a thought. Okay, here we go on another side trip.

I believe the brouhaha about Indians—or Native Americans—being insulted by the use of nicknames such as *Redskins, Braves,* and *Indians* is a case of faulty logic and is absurd.

Has none of these people ever given any thought to the reason behind choosing these nicknames? They're not meant to insult. On the contrary, they were chosen to glamorize and exalt. Look at some other team nicknames. The beauty and grace of a Tiger or a Lion stalking the jungle; the majesty of a Seahawk; an Eagle or a Falcon claiming the sky as his own; the ferocity of a Giant; the regalness of a King; the glistening image of a brilliant Cardinal.

Are men of the cloth insulted by the San Diego Padres? Has the University of Pennsylvania offended an entire religion by using the Quaker as their symbol? What about those North of the Mason-Dixon line...is use of the word Yankees an affront?

These nicknames were chosen—in some cases—a hundred years ago. They were  meant to exalt, not offend, and they should not be taken that way today. The tradition of sports in our country has enough to worry about without the added nonsense of changing team nicknames because of a small group of people rallying 'round their cause.

I know I'm politically incorrect, but, come on Indians, or Native Americans, lighten up a little. Show that you have a sense of reality.


Okay, so I had pretty much decided against a career with the Washington Redskins.

In fact, I did have a commitment elsewhere: to the Marine Corps. As part of the Marines' Platoon Leader Corps Program, I was obligated to spend two years in the Corps, but I was able to defer that for a while to take advantage of another option, that was a once-in-a-lifetime opportunity.

# CHAPTER *11*

# The Duke and I

**Hooray for Hollywood!** But I'm getting ahead of myself.

In the fall of 1953, I was contacted by a local Dodge-Plymouth dealer in Los Angeles to see if I'd be interested in doing some commercials for them.

My feeling was that if I could make an honest living doing it, I was interested, and thus began my career as a performer. At Stanford, I had majored in education, but I had a minor in speech and drama, and by then I had been interviewed many times, so I wasn't particularly terrified facing a camera.

After a few months of using my winning smile and photogenic personality to sell Dodges, I got a call from Warwick and Legler, an advertising agency with offices in L.A. It seems one of their clients had seen my commercials, and they wanted to know if I'd be interested in doing some national work.

If you're old enough, you might remember those old Vitalis commercials. The ones that warned you about that greasy kid stuff? I confess. That was me. I was their first TV spokesperson.

I also did commercials for General Nutrition Centers, which is still a going company, and for Command Shaving Cream—which is not.

I must say, I had no idea what went into making a commercial. For every 30-second commercial we see on TV, there are hours, sometimes days, of shooting and re-shooting. In addition, there are rehearsals and pre-production meetings and script changes and voice dubs and postproduction editing and sound sweetening. It's a wonder any commercials ever see the light of day.

Doing commercials was fun and financially rewarding. I still enjoy doing them today, although the calls are fewer and farther between.


I would be remiss if I didn't take note of something else that happened in 1953—something that was profoundly sad in the lack of attention it received.

While my life and career were soaring, and everything was on the ascendancy, a man died almost unnoticed. The man and I had a special bond, and it was he who had first been called The World's Greatest Athlete. His name was Jim Thorpe. Jim won the decathlon gold medal in the 1912 Olympics and was so good that even given today's training methods and diets, he would still be untouchable.

But he died with nothing.

Years after Thorpe's 1912 Olympic victory, Avery Brundage and his AAU ferrets had learned that Jim had played professional baseball in 1911 in order to feed his family. They not only took away his gold medals and trophies—but they erased his records from the books!

I had the opportunity to meet Jim a couple of times, and I can tell you he was the warmest, most sincere man who ever walked.

The stories of him having to race horses at carnivals for a few bucks are true, and I can think of no greater injustice done to anyone than what befell this great athlete and wonderful man.

If ever there was a case of *too little, too late* it was the restitution of his medals to his family years after his death.


But again I have digressed. Back to Tulare, where, on a typically cold, cloudy afternoon in December, I received a call from a Jim Fallon who had been an account executive with Warwick and

Legler, but told me he had changed jobs. I recognized the name and hoped he was calling with another series of commercials. But Jim was calling to ask me if I would be interested in playing myself in the new movie *The Bob Mathias Story.*

I don't recall how I responded, but I'm sure it was something sagacious like: "Get real, pal." Remember, two gold medals or not, a degree from Stanford notwithstanding, I was still small-town Tulare.

Besides—*what* new movie: *The Bob Mathias Story?*

But he was serious.

We met a few days later, and Jim laid out the plan for me to star in the movie along with my soon-to-be wife, Melba; each of us to play ourselves. Well, wouldn't that be easy if all I had to do was play myself?

It's funny how you remember little snippets of things that seem almost inconsequential at the time but grow in significance over the years. One of my very first thoughts was to make sure someone creditable played Coach Jackson because he had been so important a person in my life. To my delight they picked Ward Bond, and I just couldn't wait to meet him. He was the perfect coach figure: gruff and scary, but kindly and lovable.

Jim Fallon and I signed the papers to form Mathlon Productions to package the movie: a clever title combining our two names. If I thought acting in commercials was time consuming, it was nothing compared to shooting an actual movie. But it was fun. The movie was produced and distributed by Allied Artists.

I'm not sure about this, but I don't *think* it was nominated for Best Picture of 1954. That was probably because it was competing with Alfred Hitchcock's "Rear Window," Elia Kazan's "On the Waterfront" and the original "Diabolique." Just bad timing on our part. Any other year, we would've won going away! Just for the record, that's meant to be a joke!

It was interesting how people reacted to the movie. Five years prior, I had become the youngest man ever to win an Olympic gold medal. A year ago, I had become the only person ever to win back-to-back gold medals in the decathlon. But *now*, because there had been a movie about me, I was a celebrity. The movie had validated my life and my achievements, and I began getting write-ups in papers and magazines and requests for interviews outside the sports section.

And other parts of my life were heating up.

Melba and I got married in June 1954, and in July, I entered the Marine Corps as a second lieutenant.

After spending about a year in fashionable resorts such as Quantico, Virginia, and Camp Pendleton, California, I received a new assignment.

I was recruited by Harold Howland of the State Department to become America's Goodwill Ambassador to foreign lands. Little did I know I was to become "The Man Without an Address."

Howland explained that in most countries the only contact the government officials had with the United States was a formal one with embassy officials. And that the people, the citizens of most of these countries, had no contact whatsoever with Americans. It was around this time that "Yankee go home" messages were being scrawled on walls throughout the world.

The plan was for me to visit with government and local school officials in an unofficial capacity and show them what wonderful people we Americans are. Very flattering but also a little scary to think the State Department was counting on *me* to help mold the world's opinion of Americans.

From August through December 1955, I crisscrossed the globe with more than a small sense of regret. You see, on March 16, Melba had given birth to the most beautiful, most perfect baby in the history of the world. We named her Romel, and the moment I left the house to head out toward Reykjavik, Iceland, I began missing her.

The trip ended up in Honolulu, and how we got from Point A to Point B is still a blur, but I know we spent time in Ireland, Turkey, Germany, Greece, Egypt, Iraq, Iran, Pakistan, India, Indonesia, Ceylon, Hong Kong, Formosa, Japan, and the Philippines.

Typically, I would arrive at the airport where we would receive the keys to the city or the local equivalent of that ceremony. Then a motorcade would take me to my hotel. Most cities would roll out the red carpet and give me a tour of what they considered the highlights of their city. Of particular interest to me, was when I'd get the chance to visit the schools. I've always felt a particular affinity toward school kids, and, especially now that I was a father, it had even more meaning. Seeing how the various countries we visited approached the teaching process was fascinating.

Inevitably, we would end up at a stadium or a university athletic field. It seemed that every city we went to had a local champion in one or another track discipline, and I was expected to compete against him in the javelin or the hurdles or the shot put or whatever his specialty.

When we were in Istanbul, a little guy wearing a fez, a mustache as wide as his shoulders and a grin to match, beat me in the 100 meters. And did I hear about it from the State Department! "What's wrong, Bob? Are you okay, Bob? Aren't you feeling well, Bob? We're supposed to be showing these people what good athletes we are, Bob..." The State Department guy was all over me.

Finally I said: "If *we* are such good athletes, why don't you take him on in the 100?" I pointed out: "The guy ran a 10.75 for God's sake! *That's* why he beat me. My best time, even in the Olympics, was a 10.8."

The guy was a world-class sprinter, but I was never able to learn his name. But I figured I'd better get serious about this or the State Department would send me home, and I was having far too good a time.

# CHAPTER *12*

# A Teacher is Taught by His Pupils

**I was allowed to return to the states in mid-December** to be with the family for Christmas, and on the long flight from Honolulu to Los Angeles, I had plenty of time for reflection.

I had been given one of the greatest gifts anyone could ever receive. I had been given, literally, the world. I visited cities most people can only read about; I had met and touched the people. I had talked to them and listened to them talk about their lives and their countries. I had listened as they talked about their concept of America, and, to a person, when they uttered the word America, they did so with passion. Some passionately for; others against.

They had asked me about Rocky Marciano and the Rocky Mountains; about the Mississippi River and Tennessee Williams; about Texas; about New York City and about President Eisenhower's health. A woman in Chittagong, Pakistan, knew how many floors the Empire State Building had (I didn't). A teenage girl in Athens knew Thomas Jefferson had written the Declaration of Independence. A man in Baghdad wanted to know why James Madison wasn't on Mount Rushmore. A grammar school class in Kandy, Ceylon, sang the "Star-Spangled Banner" for me.

This was just the tip of the iceberg. Everywhere we went, we met people to whom we spoke—and listened.

Not everyone had kind things to say about the U.S. There were those who thought slavery was still legal. Some believed we were divided into two classes: the very rich and the very poor. When a businessman in Bombay asked me if I had an automobile I told him I did. "How did you become so wealthy at your young age?" he asked me.

When I told him I was far from wealthy, he looked at me with disgust for not leveling with him. He said, "Why do you not just tell the truth? If you are not wealthy, how can you have an automobile? Your country has paid you well for winning the Olympics, yes?"

"No," I replied. "You don't have to be wealthy in America to own a car—and the government doesn't pay us for winning Olympic medals." I went into a long explanation on how every American has the right to work and save and live his own life and, if he chooses, even go into debt to buy things.

"And the government has no control over these matters?"

They say a teacher is taught by his pupils, and that is so true. The more I talked about America, the more I learned about it and came to realize what an extraordinary country we are. I am, to this day, an unashamed patriot. I can't watch a Fourth of July parade without getting a golf ball in my throat when a high school band and color guard goes by.

It was a wonderful Christmas with our families, but more than once, my mind went to other parts of the world. I wondered what religion the man in Bombay was and if he celebrated Christmas. I hoped the girl in Athens got the Christmas present she told me she had always wanted: a plaid skirt with pleats.

After six months of rest and relaxation in the states, I headed out for another geography lesson. Between June 16 and August 18, we did the *Lisbon-down-through-Africa-around-the-Mediterranean-*

*back-through-Cairo-and-up-to-Rome-Paris-and-London tour.* Gosh, didn't everybody?

An early stop on this trip was Morocco and fabled, exotic, romantic Casablanca! I searched when we got there; oh how I searched. I peered around corners; walked the streets for hours; snuck out of the hotel in the middle of the night—but no. Scour the town as I might, I could find no trace of Bogey or Rick's American Cafe.

The next stop after Casablanca was Tunisia, where I shut down the schools. Yes, I did. The local officials had scheduled a two-day track meet to begin, the day after we arrived. About midway through the morning of the second day I realized I had been signing autographed pictures and handing them to kids since early in the morning. I asked our State Department escort: "Don't they have schools here?" When I was told the schools were closed in honor of my appearance, I couldn't believe it. It seemed frivolous then, and it seems frivolous now, to close the schools so the kids can see an Olympic athlete. A president or monarch, yes; a famous author or historian or scientist, maybe—but an athlete?

These travels were not only exciting and educational for me, but I was pleased when state department officials told me they did wonders for the U.S.'s image. It was the first contact these citizens of other countries had had with any American and, in many cases, it was the first contact any of the countries' leaders had with an American who wasn't an official representative of our embassy.

The trips served another purpose. They provided an opportunity for members of our diplomatic corps to accompany me walking the streets and visiting the schools, to meet and talk with *the people* of these countries, not just government officials, on a one-to-one basis and show them we weren't the ogres that, in some cases, their leaders had painted us as.

I summered in fashionable Taiwan where they had, of all things, a track meet. In fact, they had three track meets. On one day in particular, it was Mathias vs. Taiwan, and the last event of the day was the high jump. There was one young Taiwanese kid who just wouldn't let me get away with anything in the high jump. When I jumped 5'11", he jumped 5'11" and gave me a shy grin. When I jumped 6'2", he jumped 6'2" and smiled again. When I jumped

6'4", he jumped 6'4" and I thought I detected a snicker. When I said, "That's enough," he grinned and motioned: "Raise the bar."

After the meet, we spent some time together, and, although he spoke little English, and I certainly spoke no Chinese, somehow we were able to communicate in the language of sport and got to know each other. He was learning English in school, and, although it was painfully slow for both of us, we began corresponding after I left Taiwan. A year later, he told me he thought of me as a big brother when he came to the United States and enrolled at UCLA. His name was C.K. Yang.

In the 1960 Olympics in Rome, he and Rafer Johnson would provide one of the closest Olympic decathlon duels in history. C.K. would lose the gold medal to Rafer by only 58 points in a decathlon that came down to the last 100 meters of the last event: the 1,500 meters.

# CHAPTER *13*

# "This is the White House Calling"

**Now, while all this globe-trotting was going on,** I was leading two other lives.

Primarily, I was a lieutenant in the Marine Corps, so when I say I wasn't getting paid to be the U.S.'s Goodwill Ambassador to the world, that's not quite true. I was on the Marines' payroll as a lieutenant on active duty.

As far as being a Marine, it wasn't the worst duty I could have drawn. In fact, I can't imagine any better.

In my second life, I was making movies. In September 1956, Melba and I had moved down the road to Los Angeles to be nearer to the movie community, which seemed, at the time, to be where my future would lay.

I've already mentioned the timelessness of the classic *Bob Mathias Story* and the critical acclaim it received. Oh? I didn't? Well, trust me on that. If you ever see it in a video store, give it a try.

I was busy traveling. After *The Bob Mathias Story* was released, I received a call that actually made me do a double take. (See how I was picking up the movie jargon?)

The call was from Bob Morrison.  Now, "who," you might ask, "is Bob Morrison?"

Bob Morrison was *only* the younger brother of one of my all-time heroes.  The man they called *The Duke:* John Wayne.

It seems that Ward Bond had mentioned me to Wayne and had been kind enough to say that I had the potential to be a pretty good actor.  Wayne, at the time, was running Batjac Productions, and there was a possible opening because one of his contracted actors might be leaving.

A meeting was set up for us, and the night before we were to meet was one of the few times in my life that my mother's relaxation method didn't work for me.  This wasn't something trivial like the Olympics or traveling around the world for the State Department; I mean—I was going to meet John Wayne for God's sake!

Nervously, I drove to his office and paced in the waiting room until someone came out to get me.  When we met, as I recall, I was too tongue-tied to express the admiration I felt for him, and I just gaped and nodded when he told me he had been wanting to meet me for a long time.

Mr. Wayne confirmed there was a possibility of a position coming open in his organization. Wayne had been offered the lead in a TV series but told the producers he was *a movie guy, not a TV guy.* However, he told them he had a young actor under contract to Batjac who might be just what they were looking for for their series.

Wayne told me: "I told Jim about it, and if he wants to take a chance, I'd let him out of his contract, but I think he'd be making a big mistake.  It's a series about a sheriff or a marshall or something in some small western town; just one more Western," Wayne scoffed.

As it turned out, "Jim" was James Arness, and I got to work for Batjac Productions when Jim decided to leave to play the role of Marshall Matt Dillon in a "chancy" new TV show called "Gunsmoke."

My contract with Batjac was an excellent one that left me free to do commercials if they came along and to do movies with other companies if the opportunity was presented.

Wayne was a wonderful man.  We didn't exactly hang around together, but I did get to know him in an employee-to-boss relationship, and he had as much charisma in person as on the screen.

In fact, the John Wayne that we saw in the movies was the same John Wayne who walked our office. Tall, handsome, masculine, and an altogether imposing presence—just like on the screen.

The first movie I appeared in after *The Bob Mathias Story* was *China Doll* with Victor Mature. The only reason I was able to make this movie was because I wouldn't be training for the 1956 Olympics—a bitter pill to swallow.

My favorite governing body, the AAU, and Dan Ferris, head of the AAU as well as the International Olympic Committee, had declared me ineligible to compete because I had been paid to appear in *The Bob Mathias Story* in 1953. They did say if I was willing to return the money, I could compete. Oh sure, I still had all that money stuffed in a dresser drawer.

I guess, though, considering what the AAU did to Jim Thorpe, what I got was only a slap on the wrist, but it still hurt. I think I could have done pretty well in 1956, even though I was approaching my dotage at 25.

However, my disappointment at not being able to compete in the '56 Games was greatly ameliorated when I received a phone call one spring morning.

*Phone:* Mr. Mathias?

*Me:* Yes?

*Phone:* This is the White House calling. Hold on for the President please.

*Me* (wondering to myself): Okay, which joker is this? It must be Bob Hoegh's wife.

*Phone* (after a long wait): Good morning, Bob, this is President Eisenhower. How are you?

*Me* (recognizing the voice): I'm uh, fine, sir. How are you, sir?

*Phone:* Just fine. Let me tell you why I'm calling. I understand you won't be competing in Melbourne this summer, is that right?

*Me:* Yes sir. (Now my ego is thinking, "Wow, is Ike gonna intercede with the AAU!")

*Phone:* Well, I'm sorry to hear that, but maybe it'll work out for the best. I would like to go to the Olympics for a few days, but with all that's going on in Hungary and Poland and that part of the world, it looks like I should be sticking pretty close to home this summer. So how would like to represent me there?

*Me:* Represent you? What would that mean, sir?

*Phone:* Mostly just being there—and I guess going to a lot of dinners and stuff like that.

*Me:* (thinking: just be there and eat? I can do that.) I'd love to, Mr. President.

I got that Mr. President stuff from watching press conferences on television.

So it was settled. I would go to Melbourne as part of a three-man delegation to represent the President of the United States at the Olympics. My companions would be Dr. Sammy Lee, 1948 and 1952 Olympic Diving Champion, and the great Jesse Owens.

This started sort of a personal tradition. I have been to every Summer Olympics since 1956. Come to think of it, I haven't missed one since 1948, except for 1980, when President Carter called for a boycott of the Moscow Olympics.

I was looking forward to meeting the President. I assumed we would get together before I went to Melbourne so he could tell me his inner thoughts and state secrets; about diplomatic language, clandestine operations and the secret handshakes that heads of state use. But all I got was a plane ticket.

"Oh well."

I would eventually meet President Eisenhower, but it wouldn't be for another 10 years.

Needless to say, my first priority was to make sure I got to see the decathlon. After the event was over, and my good friend Milt Campbell climbed the top step, I felt like I was up there with him as the "Star-Spangled Banner" echoed throughout the stadium. Another good friend, Rafer Johnson, would stand on that top step in four years but now he stood just a notch below Milt, a silver medal around his neck. For the record, Vasiliy Kuznyetsov of the Soviet Union won the bronze medal.

As proud as I was to see Milt and Rafer standing there, I couldn't help but wonder how I would have done if I'd been permitted to compete.

### Frank Zarnowski:

*I don't want to take anything away from Milt Campbell, who certainly earned his title in 1956, but Bob was the logical choice (for me). I guess hindsight is always 20-20, and we are all caught up in the game of "who could have won." Bob certainly could have won had he been able to continue his track career. Natural progression would have made him a big 8,000 scorer on the 1952 table. (Milt Campbell's winning score was 7,937.)*

*Rafer (Johnson) could also have won, but he suffered a leg injury in November 1956. Rafer had won the Olympic trials, and he was the pre-meet (pre-injury) favorite in Melbourne. After all, he was the world record holder by then. Let's put it this way. Had all things gone right with Mathias' career from 1952-56, and all three (Bob, Rafer, Milt) gone to Melbourne, and all three been healthy, it could have been one of the Olympics' greatest decathlons ever. In that sort of speculation, I'd have put my money on Bob.*

*That's what could have happened. What we do know is that Milt did win. But I do know one thing: It certainly would have been a red, white, blue sweep.*

# CHAPTER *14*

# Little Screen, Big Screen

**We got home from Melbourne** just in time for my discharge from the Marines.

Like all Marines, I think, I left the Corps with mixed feelings. My travels for the State Department had been time deducted from my service, so instead of being in the Corps for the regular two years, I was in for almost two-and-a-half years. Even after my discharge I felt like I was still a Marine. In fact, even today those feelings remain. I feel as if I am still part of one of the most elite organizations in the history of the world. I don't mean elite in the sense that we were superior as individuals, but rather in the true sense of synergy. When you're a Marine, you realize that the whole is greater than the sum of its parts.

Marines are just men, like members of other armed forces, or employees of a company, or undergraduates at a university. But the discipline and the pride of belonging that the Corps instills in its members is something special—beyond special.

It's kind of like beauty. I can't define it, but I know it when I see it.

I would still be doing quite a bit of traveling as the State Department's Good Will Ambassador, and I would be making movies with Batjac, so life wasn't going to be dull.

In addition, I was becoming fascinated by politics. Since 1956 was an election year, I decided I would try my hand at campaigning. Since President Eisenhower had been good enough to send me halfway around the world, I thought I might return the favor and do some campaigning in his behalf.

Years before, in 1950, I had campaigned for Richard Nixon as a member of "Athletes for Nixon." Needless to say, in doing that I had no idea that in 1974, Nixon's Watergate problems would become, in some measure, my own problems. But more about that later.

I decided it was time to get on with my life, and, while I campaigned for Eisenhower during the summer and fall of 1956, I was also checking out some opportunities being offered.

I had left Batjac to go out and *make an honest living* and had accepted a job with the George A. Fuller Construction Company. Among other projects, they were constructing missile sites in Montana and other sparsely populated areas. It was a life I believe I would have enjoyed, had I given it more time, but I left that job after only seven months when Hollywood again pointed its finger in my direction.

Between 1956 and 1960, I was busy.

In addition to "China Doll" with Victor Mature, I was offered a television series with a man I had always admired: Keenan Wynn. I also played Theseus, son of the King of Athens in "Theseus and the Minotaur," and I played opposite Jayne Mansfield in "It Happened in Athens."

Now, I guess I don't have to tell you there wasn't an Academy Award movie in the lot, but it provided employment. It also provided some great times.

Keenan Wynn, the son of Ed Wynn, (one of America's funniest vaudevillians,) was a terrific actor and a highly effective entrepreneur. He was also a motorcycle freak.

Then there was an episode with Jayne Mansfield that has never been told before . . . stay tuned!

Keenan Wynn went everywhere on his Harley. He called me once from New York and told me he'd be in L.A. later in the week. When I asked him what day he was flying in he said: "I'm not. I'm leavin' now on the hog."

We had been working together on a TV series for NBC called "The Troubleshooters," and while Keenan is en route from New York to L.A., I'll tell you a little about the show.

It went on the air September 11, 1959, and the last episode played June 17, 1960. It could have had a much longer run but—well, I'll get to that.

Anyway, to tell you the essence of the story, I'll quote from the NBC press release summary:

> "The number-one troubleshooter of the Stenerud Corporation, a large heavy-construction firm specializing in both domestic and foreign building projects, was a grizzled old veteran named Kodiak (Keenan Wynn). He had held that post for five years, during which time he had coped with the problems involved in building highways, dams, airfields, skyscrapers and atomic installations all over the world. The pace had started to become too much for him to take, and he was in the slow process of training his assistant, Frank Dugan (Bob Mathias), to take over.
>
> "Frank was all the things that Kodiak was not—well educated, socially polished, soft-spoken, and innocent of the evil ways of the world. As the two of them traveled from assignment to assignment, they learned from each other and acquired qualities that would stand them in good stead in the future. Kodiak became somewhat less gruff and uncivilized, and Frank became stronger and more assertive.
>
> "Scotty (Bob Fortier), Skinner (Carey Lofton), Jim (Bob Harris) and Slats (Chet Allen) were crew members who made frequent appearances."

Keenan and I developed a warm friendship while we were working together, which lasted well beyond the life of "The Troubleshooters." He got me involved in motorcycle racing and almost got me killed a couple of times.

We used to go bike riding on weekends, and when there was a break on the set, we'd saddle up and take off. One of the things I didn't know about Keenan when I let him get me involved in motorcycles was that he was walking around with a steel plate in his head, the result of an accident he'd had on his bike on Wilshire Boulevard.

This had prompted him to concentrate mostly on dirt bikes, and upon occasion, we would go up to the Pear Blossom area outside of Los Angeles in California's high desert. There we would race with Lee Marvin and Bob Harris, a stuntman and cast member of "The Troubleshooters." Once, Keenan offered to pit for me in the Big Bear Mountain 50-mile race. This was less of a race than it was an obstacle course—through rivers, over cliffs and around hairpin turns. It was a three-loop course, and I did fine on the first loop. On the second loop, I started having problems when I went off the road and got stuck in a stream. Soaking wet, I got back on the course and made it to the pit, where Keenan was standing, smiling and telling me I was doing just fine.

It was the third loop that almost did me in. I was cold, sore, tired, and thinking if I never saw another motorcycle it would be fine. Midway through the loop, my front wheel hit a partially concealed rock, threw me off course and I went over a cliff. How I didn't break anything is still a mystery. Everything hurt, though, and by the time I made my way back to the roadway, I had dropped from the lead pack to near the end. By the time the race ended, I finished 105th (out of 500) and decided my racing career was over. Ended. Finished!

Now—about the ignominious ending of "The Troubleshooters." We had a single sponsor who paid the freight for the entire show, except for a few 30-second spots the NBC reps plugged in on occasion. That sponsor was Marlboro cigarettes, and it was a match made in heaven. Here we were, big, tough, macho guys solving the world's problems with our wits and our biceps. What better image for the Marlboro Man?

Keep in mind that this was back in the '50s. We knew in a vague way that smoking wasn't exactly healthy, but it was before the Surgeon General's report was published on just *how bad* it was.

Well, one day, the Marlboro representative was on the set ha-rassing all of us–Keenan in particular. This wasn't unusual. He was always on the set harassing someone.

I was a nonsmoker, so I was never in his line of fire. The others though, were always getting advice on how to hold their cigarettes, the manly way, how to reach for one, how to light it and other things one had to know in order to contract lung cancer in a manly way.

One day Keenan apparently got fed up. He told the Marlboro guy to get lost: "Go 'harass' yourself and your horse too," He used a much more graphic verb, but the message was essentially the same.

Well.

You can perhaps imagine the guy's reaction to that. Marlboro was spending a couple of million dollars a year on this TV series, and the main character tells the sponsor to go *harass* himself! We didn't know the phrase "politically correct" at the time, but this certainly was not.

Our neat little show was canceled as fast as you can say, "Bob, I have emphysema," and we were all free to go our own ways.

As it happened, I had a year remaining on my contract, so I was shipped off to Rome to play Theseus in "Theseus and the Minotaur." For those not up on Greek mythology, a minotaur is a half man, half bull (not unlike a linebacker) who went around sac-rificing young Athenian men and women by tossing them into the Cretan labyrinth. My job was to kill him, which I did, and the picture ended.

It took us nine months to shoot this picture, which had been scheduled for three months, so I was still on location in Rome when I got a call offering me the part of the American coach in a movie with Jayne Mansfield: "It Happened in Athens." This was to be shot in—of all places—Athens, so it was just a quick hop across the Adriatic. OK, here comes the Jayne Mansfield story.


No American boy with a pulse could turn down the chance to play opposite Jayne Mansfield, so after I slayed the Minotaur, I jumped on a plane to Athens.

To set the scene for this, I should tell you that ever since my Goodwill Ambassador days, traveling for the State Department, I always made it a point to visit the American embassy in whichever country I found myself. One afternoon, when I had a break from shooting, I hiked up to the embassy to pay my respects to the Ambassador and his staff.

As you might know, embassies are traditionally guarded by the Marine Corps. While I was at the embassy, I got chatting with a Marine sergeant who knew I was in town shooting the movie with Jayne.

He had a great idea. He thought the guys would love to meet Jayne if I could get her to visit the Marines barracks some evening. The word 'barracks' is used very loosely here. The Marine detachment actually occupied the top floor of an apartment building in downtown Athens.

Later, back on the set when I brought up the idea, Jayne was all for it. "That'll be fun," she said, probably visualizing a spread in *LIFE* magazine on her visit to the boys overseas. Even though most people thought of Jayne's life as a perpetual press release, she was a warm, intelligent person and genuinely cared for those she knew. Her husband, Micky Hargitay, was sort of an early-day Arnold Schwarzenegger, and he and Jayne were totally devoted to each other.

The next night after dinner, Jayne and I took a cab across town to the Marines' barracks and made our way up to their floor.

The place was so full of Marines and embassy employees that if anyone had wanted to take over the embassy that night they could have just walked in and said: "We're here, give us your files."

The boys had prepared a little snack for us in the dining room, and, as Jayne was chatting with them, her eye fell on a huge replica of the Marine globe and anchor emblem hanging on a wall. Being Jayne Mansfield, she took it off the wall and disappeared into another room with it. A few minutes later, she emerged holding the Marine emblem in front of her.

"Bet you can't guess what I'm wearing under the emblem," she taunted.

Yes they could. We all could. Jayne was wearing that which she had been born in, standing between two mirrored walls that left nothing to the imagination, and there wasn't a single eye looking directly at her!

# CHAPTER *15*

# Camp Mathias

**By now I was feeling pretty good about myself.** I had made four movies in as many years; my name was getting around Hollywood as an *actor*, not as just a jock; and even after I had tried to quit the movie business, they came after me. So now it was time to show my independence. I would hold out for better roles and higher pay.

And I would have too.

Except for four months I sat on my butt waiting for these better roles to find me. The few times the phone rang were usually invitations to play some touch football in the park. Here I was a Stanford graduate and a two-time Olympic gold medalist. But what I *really* was, was an unemployed actor.

One Sunday afternoon, I sat down and made a long list of occupations I thought I might like to pursue. Then I factored in those occupations *for which I might be suited* and the list became considerably shorter. Eventually I got down to three:

1. Coaching
2. Teaching
3. Forest ranger (I loved the outdoors and had wanted to be a forest ranger since my days as a kid at camp.)

After a few weeks of further reflection, I realized there was a pursuit that could encompass all three. Early in 1961, after searching around California for months, I found 160 acres of land in a valley that was just perfect for a boys' camp.

By using some of my own money and some borrowed money, I was able to purchase the land, and I spent the rest of the year designing the camp, clearing land and putting in bare necessities, such as building access roads and digging wells for water.

We got a few log cabins up so that we could open for the summer of 1962. Then each year after that, we added buildings, dredged the lake a little deeper and cleared the land a little further.

At first, I felt a little self-conscious about naming the camp the Bob Mathias Sierra Boys Camp, but some of my friends convinced me that my name had some meaning, and it might help attract campers.

The camp consumed me. It was my occupation, my avocation and the love of my life. When I see the way many celebrity camps are run today, with the camp's namesake making an occasional to-ken appearance to sign his trading cards, I'm very proud that at the Bob Mathias Camp, Bob Mathias was there running the camp—all the time!

After a couple of years, the camp was always filled to capacity for the full 10 weeks of summer. The boys loved it, and I loved it, and, I think if I had to pick one aspect of my life I enjoyed the most, it would be the period during which we were running the camp. Working with the kids was just great: teaching them about animals, plants, and all the other aspects of living with nature. I used to often speculate that, perhaps in an earlier day, I might have been like Henry David Thoreau and spent some prolonged time com-muning with nature in a primitive environment.

One day, while campers were arriving in their family cars, I made a discovery. A lot of the boys had sisters! I don't know why it took me so long to realize this, but the discovery led to a girls camp on the other side of the lake.

I ran the camps for 16 years, which included my tenure as a U.S. Congressman. It provided a wonderful haven from the stresses of my life in Washington, D.C. Fortunately, most of a congressman's summers are free, so I was able to continue almost a full-time role at the camp. And when I wasn't there because of Congress being in session, the campers and their parents understood.

I eventually sold the camp when I was appointed head of the U.S. Olympic Training Center and had to move to Colorado Springs. I suppose I could have kept it and made a token appearance each year, but I was never that kind of guy. I felt if the camp had my name on it, it was part of my responsibility to be there full time and take the lead in running it.

I sold it to a consortium of three men, one of whom had assisted me in running the camp. Unfortunately, they tried to diversify and expand the camp too rapidly, and they lost sight of the true business of running a summer camp: to teach kids.

They ran into major financial problems and had to bail out. The camp was then sold to the Western Diocese of the Armenian Church and is still going strong today.

# CHAPTER *16*

# Mr. Mathias Goes to Washington

**While I was actively running the camp,** my friendship with Dr. Jim Goettle and his wife Betty deepened. They had kids at the camp, and we used to spend time together during the summer and at reunions during the off-season. We'd also arrange to get together a couple of times during the year.

Jim was what we would today call an activist. He had been involved in politics as long as I had known him and eventually was named chairman of the Tulare County Republican Committee.

Partly through Jim's influence and partly because of my own convictions, I too began getting involved in politics to a small degree. Years before, I had campaigned for Richard Nixon as part of an "Athletes for Nixon" movement. I hadn't been so much a fan of Nixon as I was a believer in many of the things the Republican party stood for. I realize this was unusual for someone living in such a heavily agricultural area, but there it was.

My feelings regarding politics were, I'm afraid, somewhat naive as well as fairly idealistic. I had been brought up by my family to believe that when someone said something, he meant it. If I had known then what I got to know later, it's possible I would have never made a career move in that direction. But, as they say proverbially, that's water under the bridge—or over the dam—or wherever it is that proverbial water goes.

The thought that I should ever run for elected office was a totally foreign one. It was flattering to be able to communicate with famous politicians, such as my phone call from President Eisenhower with the ensuing opportunity to represent him at the Olympics. And because of my association with the Olympics and my duties as a goodwill ambassador, I had gotten to know quite a few politicians. Some I respected and admired; others I would put my head in an oven to avoid. But run for office myself . . . not likely.

In January 1965, we were planning the upcoming camp reunion with a committee of parents. The family and I had recently moved to Visalia, and the reunion meeting was held at Jim and Betty Goettle's house down the road a couple of miles in Tulare. After we had decided the date of the reunion and who would be doing what, like sending out invitations and other necessary stuff, Jim asked me if I would like to step outside with him.

"Why, you wanna fight?" I kidded him as we moved toward the patio door.

"No. I want *you* to fight," he said.

"You got the wrong guy, Jim," I said, "I prefer sports that don't hit me back."

"I'm serious," he said. "I'd like you to think about entering the race for Congress from our district."

"Congress!" I laughed. "Jim, for years I've been begging you to get professional help. Now it's too late."

But he didn't laugh with me.

"I'm serious, Bob. You have all the tools to make a great congressman, and you've also got vision *and* visibility. People know you and respect you."

"Sure, they know me," I said. "They know me as a guy who can run fast and jump high and smile for the camera. But respect? I don't know, Jim."

The truth is, I was flattered beyond words, but I didn't think I was qualified to be a congressman nor did I have any particular desire to be one. Most of the congressmen I had ever been exposed to were just old guys in dark suits. I knew their jobs were important to governing the country, but I was pretty much ignorant of what they did or how they did it.

Jim told me I should think about it, which I did, and the more I thought about it, the more the idea intrigued me. Over a period of a couple of weeks, my thinking evolved from *that's ridiculous* to *hmmm, maybe I could do that*, and eventually to: *I can do this!*

# CHAPTER *17*

# That Wasn't Me on the Wheaties Box

**I had some time before I had to declare** for the 1966 Congressional race, so I decided to do some digging about what this congress thing would be all about.

Al Elliott was the head of the Tulare County Fair. He was also a former Democratic congressman from our district, so I made up reasons to spend time with Al and pick his brain. For obvious reasons, I was a little circumspect in my conversations with Al, but he was the type of man to whom I don't think it would have mattered. Even though he was a Democrat, and I was (leaning toward being) a Republican, he spoke freely to me of his experiences in, and running for, Congress. He told me what it took to run for election, what would be expected of me, what I would need in the way of staff and financial backing, and—most important—if I won, what the life of a Congressman was all about.

I have to admit there were a couple of times during our many conversations that I pretty much decided that the congressional life wasn't for me. At one point, Al even said: "Bob, if you ever think of running for a public office, I think you'll probably win, but I'm not sure you'll be happy."

When I asked him why, he said simply: "There's a lot of bags in public office—sleaze bags, scum bags, and wind bags and you seem to have an allergy to all three."

I took that as a compliment and continued my quest for information. I think by that time, though, deep down, I had already convinced myself to make a run at the office. I just hadn't yet realized it.

I met with Jim Goettle often, and, although he never said it, he knew I was going to run. Years later, when he told me about it, I asked him how he knew.

"You kept asking me about committee assignments," he said. "A guy who's indifferent to running doesn't dig so deep about that stuff."

He was probably right. I remember asking him, and anyone else I knew who might have any information, on how Congress was run and on how the committee assignments worked. I wanted to be on the Foreign Affairs Committee, and I remember when I first got into Congress I was assigned to the Agriculture Committee because of having been raised in such a heavy farm area like California's central valley.

Agriculture was okay. In fact, I enjoyed it. After all, I had spent most of my life with farmers, and I felt I had a lot to offer, but I still wanted to be on Foreign Affairs. I was sure all the traveling I had done for the State Department and meeting heads of foreign states would be good background for that committee.

But I'm getting ahead of myself. There was still the matter of a formal decision—to run or not to run, then to figure out how to get elected. One major consideration was the fact that the 18th Congressional district was about 60-percent Democratic.

It was June 1965, after exhaustive conversations with a lot of people who had become friends and advisors, that I decided to make a run. I told no one but my immediate family, because you see, I had already become a little shifty myself.

Let me explain.

Ever since the '48 Olympics, I had been receiving a constant stream of invitations from all across the country to make speeches at schools, veterans groups, service clubs, women's organizations and the like. I was always glad to do this, and when I spoke, I spoke in mostly platitudes. Over the years, I had come to know what the audiences wanted to hear. Men's groups wanted to hear stories about the Olympics and life in the Marines; women wanted me to tell them about Victor Mature and John Wayne, and what it's like to be in the movies.

Now, I was not going to wait for invitations to make speeches. I decided this was just like sports, and the better I prepared myself for the competition, the better I would do. I hired a group of people whose job was to contact organizations within the district and tell them I was going to be in their town and would be available to speak to them.

I told many of the same stories over and over, but because I always spoke to different audiences, the stories were always fresh. Now I was going to concentrate on my district, which encompassed Kern, Kings and Tulare counties. I would tell of the excitement of winning an Olympic gold medal; assure my audience that John Wayne in person was just like the John Wayne in the movies; tell them (peacetime) war stories from the Marine Corps and infer that Victor Mature and Jayne Mansfield just couldn't wait to see me the next time I was in Hollywood.

When the inevitable comment came from someone in the audience that he or she remembered my picture on the Wheaties box, I would smile my most charming smile and say: "That wasn't me on the Wheaties Box."

I never could figure out why, but people always thought—and still think to this day—that I was on the Wheaties box. Actually, it was my friend, Bob Richards, the incredibly gifted pole vaulter.

During these speeches, I smiled until my face cracked; I was friendly, helpful, courteous, kind, etc., but I was never overtly political.

I answered every question put to me honestly, but I also managed to steer the questions into an area we had never entered before: local problems and opportunities.

Around this time, the Soviet bloc countries were beginning to eat us up in international competition. It was well-known that their athletes were subsidized by the state, and the question invariably came up. "Would the United States eventually subsidize *our* athletes?"

This was made to order for me. I was able to give a vague, noncommittal answer, then neatly switch the subject from *athlete* subsidies to *farm* subsidies.

Wow!

Did *that* get their attention.

Remember, we're talking about cotton and dairy farmers as well as fruit and vegetable growers in the heart of America's greatest agricultural region.

The strategy was based on the fact that I was not officially a candidate for Congress or any other office, so no matter what I did, where I did it or whatever I said, the media would report what I was saying with no obligation to give others equal time.

In effect, I was campaigning like crazy throughout the district, but the opponent I would face in November didn't know it—and if he did, there was nothing he could do about it. That is, if he even cared.

Harlan Hagen was the Democratic incumbent in the 18th and after seven terms was pretty firmly entrenched (read complacent)— which led to hope for me. So firmly ensconced was he, in fact, he rarely ever visited the district. When he came home on recess, he just came home. Period. And the little campaigning he did, he was mostly going through the motions. He didn't realize at the time how vulnerable he had made himself through his inattention to his constituents, but once the campaign began, it became pretty obvious that he hadn't been tending to the business of getting reelected.

The last bit of business I had to attend to before officially declaring myself a candidate was to round up a staff.

# CHAPTER *18*

# On the Campaign Trail

**Someone told me about a professional campaign manager** living in Toluca Lake, down in the Los Angeles basin. His name was Bob McGee, and he had a terrific reputation, both for winning campaigns *and* for integrity. At least I knew enough to find an honest guy to run my campaign. After calling three wrong Bob McGees in L.A., I finally got his number from someone.

When I introduced myself there was a silence, then he said: "Who is this really?"

When I repeated myself he asked: "Bob Mathias, the movie star?"

I was already in love with Bob McGee.

I finally convinced him that I was running for Congress, and we agreed to get together later that week to talk about him managing my campaign. We reached an agreement almost immediately; and he began working on the strategy and putting a staff together.

The strategy was as simple as could be. I was going to travel the district nonstop, speaking at every Rotary Club and ladies flower arrangement society in existence in the 18th Congressional District. Now that I was a declared candidate, the gloves were off. I was ready to do head-to-head battle with Harlan Hagen. I immediately challenged him to a series of debates on the issues of the day.

But a funny thing happened. He debated me once and then apparently decided I wasn't a serious contender, so he ignored me. Meanwhile, McGee was busy putting together a newspaper ad campaign featuring me as the bright new savior, and for comparison, he found a picture of Harlan that must have been taken after an all-night binge or something. (Actually, I don't know if Harlan even drank, but this picture looked like he'd been out all night with the boys.)

I should mention how different campaigning was in those days. We used television, but not the way it's used today. We used it primarily in news coverage. McGee would invite the local news people to a speech and hope they would bring a camera and give us some time during their 11 o'clock newscast that night. We did create two TV commercials that were used near the end of the campaign but very judiciously because of the cost.

Our primary media for exposure were newspapers and personal appearances. McGee set up a network of city and county chairmen, who arranged for me to speak at various functions during the campaign. The appearances were supposed to be coordinated so I could get to each one with enough travel time in between. It was McGee's job to see to that, and, most of the time, he did. However, there were those days that we had maybe a half hour to get from the Visalia Lions Club breakfast to the Fresno Women's Sodality meeting, a distance of about 40 miles over country roads.

"Bob," I would whine, "how can we do this?"

"We can't," he would reply. "That's why we have the high school band—to kill time 'til we get there."

"Okay." He was the manager. I was just the candidate.

I learned quickly that I enjoyed campaigning. I thought back to the day in 1948 when I gulped and stuttered my way through a thank you speech in Tulare and couldn't believe that I would now get up in the morning impatient to get in front of the people and tell them about my plans for the district. I also enjoyed meeting people and getting their views on things.

What I hated, was what is perhaps the most important function of any campaign. The raising of funds. I was temporarily relieved when McGee laid out the staff structure, and I saw we would have a finance chairman. I thought it would be his job to raise the money we needed, but he was just there to keep track of the money and handle the reporting.

I found it extremely distasteful to have to get on the phone and call people to ask them for money. We did a lot of what would today be called *networking*. We held fund-raising dinners, coffee klatches, lunches, and set up other functions to raise money, but it always came down to asking for it.

I'm sure most candidates feel the same way. No one likes to ask for money. Some are just better at covering up their distaste than others.

We had a saying: "Shake a hand, shake loose a vote." And it was true. There was nothing like personal contact to sway a voter into your corner.

After all, we were called representatives. That meant our job was to represent the people of our district. In order to do that we *had* to know their feelings on matters that concerned them.


Television has created disturbingly linear, one-way communications. It is highly efficient at reaching voters, therefore extremely important in today's overall campaigns. But it's so expensive that today's candidates have to spend most of their time raising money to pay for it. To raise money, they go where the money is: to wealthy contributors and simpatico organizations. Because of all the time they have to spend on fund-raising, they don't have time to get out into the district and hear what their constituents think about matters.

The average representative today is representing his constituents by reading surveys to see what they think. I believe a great deal of communications is lost when the representative is not in the district listening to the voters but is in his office listening to the lobbyists.

When is the last time you actually met a candidate face-to-face?

Sadly, what is lost is the ability of the citizen to influence the candidate. I hate to tell you how many times I caught hell from voters after I was elected. When someone didn't like how I voted on a certain bill I sure heard about it the next time I ran for election.

All this is not to say TV is bad; it's just taken so much of the personal contact and opportunity for two-way communications out of election campaigns. But it needn't be that way.

Every television and radio station in the country is licensed by the Federal Communications Commission. It would be easy for the FCC to eliminate the candidate's need to sacrifice input from his constituency in favor of raising money for television. The FCC could simply mandate that all TV and radio stations commit a certain block of time, equally distributed and free of charge, to major candidates for public office.

That would permit candidates to run their TV and radio campaigns at little or no cost and return to them the ability to go out into their districts and communicate with their constituencies.

Would it hurt the stations?

Probably a little. They would certainly lose some advertising revenue, but they already provide airtime for public service announcements, so this could be included as part of that program. This plan could also serve another purpose. It could narrow the window during which political commercials would run and make the campaigns blessedly shorter.

And a still further benefit is that the candidates would become a lot better informed on the issues that are important to their constituency. I remember getting a hell of an education from the voters. I started out telling them what I was going to do and ended up listening to them tell me what I *should* do. Just by listening, I became an *expert* on about 200 subjects I had known little or nothing about before running for Congress.

The adage that a teacher is taught by his pupils is never more true than when applied to politics.

# CHAPTER *19*

# Welcome to Washington

**One of the benefits of running for office** was that I finally got to meet former President Eisenhower. He had an office near Palm Springs, and three of the California candidates for Congress, Jerry Pettis from Loma Linda who was running in the 33rd Congressional District, Chuck Wiggins from El Monte's 25th Congressional District and I, spent a day with Ike having our pictures taken. Ike was an extremely gracious and unassuming man. I had admired him for many years, so actually meeting him was a special treat.

Winning the election was almost anticlimactic. By the time election day came around, I almost didn't care whether we won or lost. The important thing was that the campaigning was over. Remember I said I enjoyed campaigning? I did, but it was exhausting.

I can't imagine what it must be like today for presidential candidates, jetting from one place to another—breakfast in Providence then a drive to Boston for a quick speech; lunch in Indianapolis with a quick side trip to address the Notre Dame faculty in South Bend; dinner in Seattle—down to San Francisco for a plane-side photo-op, then to L.A. for a strategy session and fund-raiser. In bed after midnight and up at 4:30 the next morning to be in Denver for breakfast at seven.

And because of television's relentless eyes and ears, the candidate needs a different speech addressing different issues for each stop . . . and he doesn't *dare* look fatigued.

Our winning margin was 56 percent, a tribute to Bob McGee's great organizing abilities, and Harlan Hagen's inattention to the campaign.

I might not have been the world's most dramatic orator, but I stuck with the issues, and when I didn't know the answer to a question, I would say so, find it out and mail or call the person who asked it.

During the campaign, I had pretty much ignored my camp, so I spent a good part of November in the Sierras tending to things that had to be done. We had to expand the sewer system and bring in more water, and there was always maintenance needed on the cabins and around the grounds. So the time between election day and the swearing in ceremony passed pretty quickly.

In early December, I flew to Washington for a new members orientation session and, of course, the all-important *office lottery draw.*

Congressional offices are assigned by seniority; the best offices going to the most senior members. New members do not inherit the office of the man they succeed. Rather, a member with seniority gets to move into it if he wishes. Each new member's name goes into a lottery, and he gets to select his office based on how early his name is picked. I was lucky and got a pretty good draw and got to pick an office in the Longworth House Office Building. There were three office buildings in which members had their offices: Cannon, Longworth and the newest one, the Sam Rayburn House Office Building.

The orientation session was daunting. There was so much to learn, not the least of which was how to find our way around the

Capitol. They told us about the difference between the bells for quorum calls and the bells for a vote. They told us how to find the underground tram that would take us to our office from the Capitol Building. They told us about staffing, how the voting system worked, how to introduce a bill, how to amend a bill, where the cafeterias were, places to look for housing, and so on.

By the time they were finished, my head was swimming with facts.

The orientation sessions were held by the leaders of Congress, and it was a time to get to know people I had only read about up to then. There were the leaders, there were the returning members, and there were us "freshmen." The main difference between being a freshman in college and a freshman in Congress is age. Other than that, we were as wide-eyed as kids going to the circus for the first time.

I remember being warmly greeted by Gerry Ford, who was then the Minority Leader. His first words to me were something like: "Welcome. It's about time you decided to do something worthwhile with your life."

I always felt a certain affinity toward Ford, and I assume the feeling was reciprocated. Gerry had been an All-American center at the University of Michigan, and we became good friends based to a large degree on our sports backgrounds.

After the orientation sessions ended, we all went home and tried to prepare as best we could for the next two years when we would be known, collectively, as the 90th Congress.

Mom and Dad flank Bob, the high school track whiz. Who could've known then...?

Photo courtesy of Bob Mathias Collection

The man without whom maybe none of this would have happened: Bob's high school coach and mentor, Virgil Jackson (left). In May of 1948, they were both wondering how Bob was going to compete with world-class athletes in two months' time.

Photo courtesy of Bob Mathias Collection

THE

Bob Mathias

STORY

THE Bob Mathias STORY

Bob's very first decathlon, 7th Annual Pasadena Games (held in Los Angeles Memorial Coliseum, June 1948.) Bob sits in the middle. Facing the camera (left to right) are Al Lawrence (LAAC), Ross Winton, and Don Winton (LAAC). With their backs to the camera (left to right) are Dick Nash, *L.A. Mirror,* and Doc Haines (AAU). Floyd Simmons is kneeling behind Doc Haines.

Photo courtesy of Bob Mathias Collection

The ultimate thrill! The World's Greatest Athlete, 17-year-old Bob Mathias, stands on the top step after conquering the field in the 1948 Olympic decathlon. Fellow American Floyd Simmons was third, while Ignace Heinrich of France placed second.

Photo courtesy of Bob Mathias Collection

Photo courtesy of Bob Mathias Collection

President Truman does a double handshake with Olympic champions Bob Mathias (left) of Tulare, California, and Arthur Cook of Washington, D.C., at the White House. Mathias, 17, won the decathlon, and Cook, 20, captured the rifle marksmanship title at the London games.

THE

STORY

THE Bob

Bob Mathias

STORY Mathias

National Championship, June '49:

"Mom, I won the Olympics last year and I've just won the world championship. Now they have to stop calling me 'The kid' ... don't they?"

Photo courtesy of Bob Mathias Collection

Photo courtesy of Bob Mathias Collection

Bob Mathias, clutching the trophy he was awarded for winning the U.S. decathlon championship with a record performance at Tulare, California, July 2, is surrounded by youngsters as he leaves the Tulare High School stadium. Mathias rang up a total of 7,825 points under a new scoring system, eclipsing his record of 7,444 points, figured by using the same system.

THE

STORY

THE Bob Mathias STORY

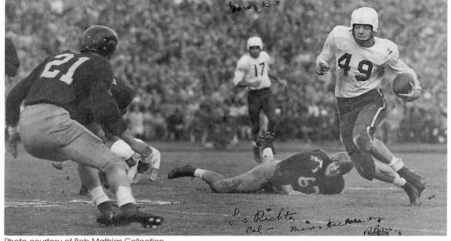

Bob Mathias (49) eludes Les Richter (67), two-time All American, during The Game—Stanford vs. California, 1951.

Winning an Olympic gold medal has certain side benefits. Bob with actresses Debbie Reynolds (left) and Celeste Holm in Acapulco, 1953.

THE

Mathias

Bob

STORY

THE Bob Bob

STORY Mathias

Yes, there actually was a Pop Warner. He is seated on the right and is paid due homage by Bob (center) and a USC athlete in 1953.

Photo courtesy of Bob Mathias Collection

Photo courtesy of Bob Mathias Collection

This is the guy who was on the Wheaties box? Invariably, whenever Bob appears at a speaking engagement, someone will say, "I remember when you were on the Wheaties box." He never was. It was pole-vaulter Bob Richards (right).

THE Bob Mathias STORY

Welcome to the corps. Bob being sworn into the U.S. Marine Corps, January 13, 1954.

*Semper Fi!* Lt. Robert Bruce Mathias, U.S. Marine Corps, 1955.

THE

STORY

THE

STORY

Bob

Mathias

Bob

Mathias

"If one Mathias is good, two Mathiases must be better." Bob with senator Charles "Mac" Mathias of Maryland, 1970.

Photo courtesy of Bob Mathias Collection

Photo courtesy of Bob Mathias Collection

"You see, Mr. President, this is about the height of a high hurdle..." Bob with Ike during one of his congressional campaigns.

Photo courtesy of Bob Mathias Collection

Two ex-jocks. Bob chats in the Oval Office with a former All-American center from the University of Michigan, President Gerald Ford.

THE

STORY

Bob Mathias

THE Bob Mathias STORY

Bob addresses a congressional meeting during the formation of the U.S. Olympic Training Center. NFL coach George Allen looks on.

Photo courtesy of Bob Mathias Collection

Photo courtesy of Bob Mathias Collection

Talk about two guys in the wrong line of work... Two Bobs, Mathias and Cousy, defend against their opponents on the tennis court.

Photo courtesy of Bob Mathias Collection

"One of the wonderful things about grandchildren is that they are guaranteed to be the most beautiful children the world has ever seen." Top row (left to right): Sara, Lucas, Chance, and Alex. Bottom Row: Eza, Max, Haven, Jordan, and Elijah.

THE Bob Mathias STORY

THE Bob Mathias STORY

# CHAPTER 20

## Meeting People With "Names"

**On January 3, 1967, we convened** for the first time as a body. Some of the people I met were already legends, such as Speaker of the House John McCormick. Some of the names were those I had been reading about for years, such as Mel Laird. Some, like George Bush, still had their more famous years ahead of them.

### George Bush:

*Bob Mathias was a big star in our freshman class. When the class first met following the 1966 election, everyone knew who Bob was; everyone instantly liked him.*

*He was a good conscientious member of Congress. He worked hard and looked after his district well.*

*I liked Bob a lot—still do.*

My first impression of living in Washington was that I couldn't afford to live in Washington. A Congressman in 1967 earned the munificent salary of $22,500, which, in 1967 dollars wasn't as bad as it sounds. It was probably the equivalent of $50,000 or $60,000 in 2000. Not slave wages by any means  but still not enough to maintain two homes. We had to sell our house on Myrtle Avenue in Visalia, so when we came home on vacation, or I came back to visit the district, my parents' house in Tulare was our base.

We found a nice house on Walters Woods Road, in Falls Church, Virginia, which was a reasonable commute to the Capitol.

One of the first orders of business was to elect the Congressional leaders. I was proud to cast my very first Congressional vote for Gerald Ford to continue as my party's leader.

The next order of business was committee assignments. At one particular meeting, Ford suggested that George Bush, Jack Kemp and Bob Mathias be assigned to the *Committee on Aging Jock Affairs,* Bush being a former All-American first baseman from Yale and Kemp having been the outstanding quarterback for the Buffalo Bills. As I recall the session, we agreed to serve but only if Ford would become Chairman Emeritus.

As I mentioned earlier, I was assigned to the Agriculture Committee with a vague promise from the leadership that when an opening came up on Foreign Affairs, I would be considered. As it turned out, the nation's agricultural scene—especially in the state of California—was beginning to get interesting.


A child born in 1927 into a family of migrant farm workers in Yuma, Arizona, had left the farms to become active in labor organizations and to champion the plight of itinerant farmworkers. Cesar Chavez had successfully organized and founded the national Farm Workers Union in 1962 and, with the support of the AFL-CIO and other unions, was now working on organizing California's grape pickers. We were still three years away from the massive grape boycotts, but there was a great deal of unrest throughout the entire central valley.

In my first meeting with Chavez' people, I felt tremendous conflicts as I listened to his point of view. There was no question that the pay and working conditions of the migrant farm worker were appalling. On the other hand, didn't my allegiance lay with the farmers of the district who had elected me? I was their representative in Congress. The farm owners had sent me to Washington to represent them, and their interests were diametrically opposed to the workers.

What position should I take?

I was philosophically opposed to unions. At one time, they had unquestionably served a purpose. The pay scale and working conditions that American laborers endured in the early part of the century were unforgivable, and the unions did a great deal to correct that. But now union leaders were fat cats; more concerned about their own personal wealth and well-being than the conditions of their rank and file.

On the other hand, weren't the conditions under which the migrants worked comparable to those of, say, the coal miners of the '20s and '30s?

Was I to listen to my conscience telling me to side with the migrant farm workers, or was I to listen to my other conscience telling me to support those whom I represented in Congress?

I felt an almost unbearable sadness for the workers because I had seen their conditions as I was growing up, but as it was pointed out to me, I didn't represent them. They were here today, in El Centro tomorrow and back in Mexico next week.

The fact that they weren't American was never a factor in my thinking. They were, for the most part, legal aliens and they were forced to make a living under terrible conditions. And they were represented by their union—supposedly.

A series of unrelated events helped me decide my position on the matter.

A group of us on the Agriculture Committee had been attending meetings in the various farm belts throughout the country, and the last one was held in Sacramento. That meeting finished up late on a Thursday night, and I decided, rather than fly back to Washington the next morning, I would rent a car and drive down to Tulare to spend the weekend with my parents.

Monday morning, I drove up to the San Francisco International Airport. The ticketing agent recognized me and, since the flight was half empty, offered me a free upgrade to first class. I accepted it with thanks and sank back in the luxury of first-class leather.

About a half hour into the flight, the man across the aisle leaned over and asked: "Aren't you Bob Mathias?" I admitted I was, and he introduced himself. "You remember me, don't you?" he asked.

His name was familiar, and he was wearing the clothes of a farmer, so I thought maybe I had met him at one of the Agriculture Committee meetings.

We chatted across the aisle for awhile, and then he asked me what my feelings were regarding the farm workers union. Then it clicked in my mind, and I realized where I knew him from. He was Cesar Chavez' right-hand man, and we had met as well as having spoken on the phone.

As we made small talk, he told me his reasons for going to Washington, but my mind was elsewhere. I was flying first class by the grace of a generous ticket agent. But why was he there? I decided to ask him, and his answer went a long way to making up my mind in favor of the farm owners and against the union.

"Did you get bumped up into first class?" I asked.

He answered with a flip of his wrist: "I always fly first class."

"It's pretty expensive, isn't it?"

"What's money?" he said, "We have half the money in the world."

"Where do you get it?"

He looked at me like I was a child asking why water is wet. "From the workers' dues and a whole bunch of rich people who support the union."

# CHAPTER *21*

# Term Limits?
# The Debate Continues

**So, while I was very sympathetic** to the problems of the farm workers, I felt there was no way I could support their union.

Later on in my first term, I met another of Chavez' key people: Dolores Huerta. She was a bright and charming lady who did her best to convince me that I should back the union. She sat in my office for hours one afternoon and laid out a logical, sensible case for the union, but as far as I was concerned, the farm owners were businessmen, and the farms were their businesses. It was up to them to decide what were affordable wages, and I knew for a fact that most of them were in the process of improving the working conditions for their laborers. They were permanent residents of my district. They needed my support, and, even if I sound like a broken record, they had sent me to Congress to represent them, and if I did otherwise, I would have been breaking faith.

I know this might come across as heresy because Cesar Chavez is practically a religious icon to some, but as far as I could see, the battle between the farmers and Chavez' group was strictly one for public opinion, and both sides were intent on Congress and the press approving *their* position.

I was asked by a delegation of farmers if there was anything they could do to get a favorable image in Congress after Chavez' blitz PR campaign had organized *Boycott Grapes* groups all over the country. "Since you have so many grapes," I suggested, "why not send a basket of grapes to each member of Congress with a note explaining *your* position?" They did just that and were surprised when most Democrats in the house returned the grapes.

Even though Congress was run largely along party lines, there was a great deal of camaraderie—off the floor—among members of different political persuasions. I've heard Congress described as a men's club, which it isn't, but given the nature and personality of most of the members, and what it takes to become a congressman, it is sort of an elite association of overachievers.

Some members were as friendly and as helpful as can be; some were always wound so tight I was afraid they might explode. Others wouldn't give you the time of day in the hallway unless it would benefit them in some way. But for the most part, I enjoyed the associations and tried to get along with everyone. My neighbor, two doors down in the Longworth Building, was Ed Edwards, a Democratic Congressman from Louisiana. Ed and I had practically nothing in common, except we were both freshmen and took our jobs seriously. We were rarely on the same side of an issue, and often we would visit late into the night trying to convince the other of our point of view—or in some cases, trying to understand the other's point of view. After serving a couple of terms in Congress, Ed ran for, and won, the governor's seat in Louisiana.

Although the Congressional salary wasn't flamboyant, there were no restrictions on how much we could earn outside. Many Congressmen were from wealthy families or had run for Congress after successful business careers, so their income wasn't much of an issue. I didn't fall into either of those categories, but I did have income from outside sources. The camp was providing me a nice living, and I was often sought to make appearances at retail grand openings, professional and college games, and other events. In addition, I was doing a series of promotions for *Sports Illustrated,* which provided additional income.

Additional money was fairly easy to come by to all members of Congress. There were always companies and organizations soliciting members to address their annual meeting or other event. When one made these speeches, all expenses were paid as well as an honorarium. The honorarium usually was only a couple of hundred dollars, but there were times when some younger members needed those dollars for rent. For obvious reasons, when a representative made a speech in his own district, he did not accept compensation.

These speaking engagements, for the most part, had no strings attached. I mean, there were no favors asked, and none were expected. It was strictly a business arrangement where a group needed a speaker, and they hired one. It's almost certain that wasn't always the case, but I know I personally was never offered any sort of inducement of value to sway my vote.

That's not to say a congressman isn't constantly bombarded by various special interest groups, lobbyists and others seeking to influence his vote. That goes on all the time, and it comes with the territory. Sit in Congress for two years, and you'll see every sort of mind-swaying technique, short of the rack, known to man.

One of the perks of Congress from my point of view was all the time off we got. I was lucky in that Congress adjourns for a month each summer, which allowed me to run my camp. For most of that time, I could be in my wilderness at the camp yet still be close enough to my constituency so that in an election year, I could make daytrips down into the valley to campaign.

And speaking of perks: Congress has many others.

One is the ability to "frank" their mail. That is, to send mail without postage. I felt a little guilty about that at first, but one of my colleagues pointed out: "Look, we're running the damn country for less than 25 grand a year. We can at least let them pay our postage. Besides, it's just a case of the money going out of one pocket and into the other anyway."

It sounded logical, and I was sending a lot of mail back into the district, so I used the franking privilege without guilt.

But when it comes to congressional perks, franking is one of the minor ones. Free (first-class) air travel, free medical care, and a pension after five years of service are not minor; in fact, they're pretty significant.

Some of the others, like subsidized haircuts and free parking, are great conveniences, but the one that attracted me first as a freshman congressman was the access to the congressional stationery room. At first blush that doesn't sound very exciting, but just think about being able to get not only note pads, letterheads, pens and pencils but also crystal ashtrays, coffee mugs, flower vases, dishes and other great things—all with that wonderfully distinctive House of Representatives seal.

All these wonders were available through the House stationery room, and, while it wasn't free, the prices were very low, and each congressman got a stationery and supplies allowance, that was more than enough to keep him and his extended family well stocked. I remember sending coffee mugs to a lot of friends and relatives.

It's easy to see why some Congressmen are loathe to ever leave office. Congress has voted itself raise after raise, so today the pay is way better than in the '60s and '70s. It's one of the best jobs in the world with plenty of opportunities to legally make lots of money above and beyond the congressional salary so—why leave?

Why indeed?

Many people are asking this question from both sides of the argument, and it has become a national conundrum: *Term Limits or not Term Limits?*

Here's what I think:

Limit senators to two six-year terms and members of the House to five terms. That's 12 years for senators and 10 years for congressmen. That's more than enough for a congressman to accomplish what he went to the Capitol for. Then let him leave in favor of a new man with new ideas. I knew and worked with men who made Congress a career. For the most part, they had lost touch with their constituencies, were low on energy, were tied into special interest groups and were totally predictable in their voting patterns.

Congress *needs* constant transfusions of new blood. Imagine a team that takes on no new players. Within a few years, they'll be getting blown out of the game by everyone they play. New team members always make the team better—always. New Congressmen always make Congress better.

There are a lot of arguments against term limits:

*If we had term limits, bills would be written by professional bureaucrats.*

Not true. I listened to my constituents as do most congressmen until they get too caught up in themselves. If you listen, you know what the voters in your district want, and that's something no agency employee knows.

*If we had term limits, we wouldn't have the professionals in Congress to help steer the country and the young congressmen.*

It takes just a few weeks to get the feel of Congress. Once you've gone through the orientation, you know *where* things are. Within a few weeks of that, you learn *how* things work. *That's* what you need to know to represent your district. There are no deep secrets to governing. Be honest, listen to the voters, and do what you think is right.

*Our system of biennial congressional elections is a term limit system in itself.*

This is the most dangerous of all misconceptions about term limits. Unless you've been there, you have absolutely no idea how difficult it is to unseat the incumbent. He has so many advantages! Incumbents have the connections, they have endorsements from party leaders, they're known in their district. They accumulate favors from people and groups with money. They still have all the perks of Congress, and most important—*they have almost unlimited access to campaign funding.* A phone call from an incumbent Congressman to a special interest group to whom he has been friendly will bring immediate financial support.

In some districts, incumbents are so firmly entrenched, they would have to be guilty of a crime to lose an election—in fact, there have been congressmen who actually were criminals who still got reelected.

It was during my tenure in Congress that the House had to vote on whether or not to seat Harlem Congressman Adam Clayton Powell. There wasn't much separating this guy from a thug on the street, but his district kept reelecting him.

Finally, things got so bad, and his actions became so blatant, that the House became embarrassed and voted not to seat him at the start of the 90th Congress.

About midway through my first term, I was fooling around in the gym one evening and twisted the wrong way. It felt like someone had ripped part of my back away. I had heard guys complain about back pain and sympathized with them, but to myself I always thought: *"How bad can a little back pain be?"*

Now I knew. I went down to my knees and could only stand up by leaning against something. Somehow, I got to my car, drove home and got into bed. Sleeping was impossible, because every time I moved, a knife raked down my back. The next morning, by leaning against things, I managed to struggle into the shower. I just let the hot water run on me until things loosened up a little. After a while, I was able to get dressed with some difficulty. Until it came to putting on my socks. That took about 40 minutes.

Going to work was out of the question, and I headed right to the House doctor's office. He gave me some muscle relaxer pills and some exercises to do after the pain subsided a little. He also took me to a machine on the Senate side, which acted as a traction device for the neck. He wanted me to take some painkillers too, but I've always felt that if something is hurting me, it's for a reason. I didn't want to silence my body, so I passed on the codeine.

I was religious about going to the gym and working on the neck-pulling machine. One night, while I was stretching out, I noticed a guy in one of the whirlpools. He looked familiar and I knew that I knew him from somewhere, but sitting naked in an oval tub full of bubbles, his face didn't connect to anything. However, recognition came quickly when he greeted me with: "Good evening, Mr. Mathias."

I immediately responded: "Good evening, Senator Dirksen." At that time, there was no voice in the nation as recognizable as that sugary baritone of Senator Everett Dirksen of Illinois.

Months later, I began to get friendly with George Bush, who, as I mentioned earlier, had been an outstanding athlete at Yale. After my back was back to normal, George challenged me to a game of paddleball. I had never played before, but I had watched some of the members play on occasion. Paddleball, for God's sake—how challenging could it be?

After running me all over the court for a half hour or so and whipping me properly, our future president looked at me with mock disgust and muttered: "World's greatest athlete, huh?" I could only hang my head.

I'm aware that I'm beginning to sound like a shameless name-dropper, but another person whom I got to know better in Washington was someone I had served with on the Sears Roebuck Sports Advisory staff in the '50s and early '60s. He was a former player for the Boston Red Sox by the name of Ted Williams. Others on that staff were Buddy Young the football player, Tony Trabert the tennis star, and Sir Edmund Hilary of Mt. Everest fame.

Ted was batting coach for the Washington Senators (the baseball team, not the other house of Congress). He also volunteered to help out at the annual Donkeys verses Elephants baseball game, that once-a-year event in which it was permissible for Congressional Democrats and Republicans to go at each other with wooden clubs.

When Ted and I were together at Sears, we used to have discussions about what was the toughest thing to do in sports. His contention was: "The single most difficult thing to do in sports is to hit a home run," he said. "You have to hit a tiny baseball that's traveling over 90 miles an hour, dipping and jumping and doing all sorts of things as it approaches you. You have to hit it dead square on and with enough power to put it over a wall 400 feet away."

I took the position that the single most difficult act in sports is to set a world record. I said: "Every time a world record is set, the standard is raised higher, making it even more difficult for the next guy who comes along to break it."

This was a floating argument that went on for years whenever Ted and I would get together.

The night of the Congressional baseball game, Ted was coaching at first base, and in my first time at bat I hit the first pitch deep to center field; so deep, in fact, that it bounced once and went into the stands for a ground rule double. As I trotted to first I smiled at Ted and said: "That was one of the easiest things I ever did."

His hat in hand, Ted Williams bowed deeply as I rounded the base.

I know he meant it as a joke, but I still remember the night Ted Williams removed his cap and bowed to *me* on the baseball field.

Speaking of Ted Williams, there are certain athletes who combine their athletic talents with a certain charisma that makes them very special. They only come along once or twice in a generation, and if you're lucky, maybe you'll get to see one of them perform at his peak. Williams was one. Joe DiMaggio was another; Babe Ruth, Lou Gehrig, Jim Brown, Carl Lewis, Bob Cousy, Magic Johnson, Yogi Berra, Michael Jordan... .

There are others but not many. Recently, I was having dinner with a friend, and we were discussing the difference in sports today as opposed to when we were kids. We agreed that one of the main differences is money. Another is the fact that the major leagues in all sports have expanded to the point where the talent has been drastically diluted. My friend asked me: "Based on the salaries in Major League Baseball today, with back-up outfielders who hit .255 making a million dollars, what do you think they'd have to pay DiMaggio or Williams?"

The answer was easy. "Everything east of the Mississippi."

There's a wonderful story about Babe Ruth that might be apocryphal. In 1929, at the height (or depth) of the Great Depression, a sportswriter pointed out to him that his salary of $80,000 was more than the president's that year. "How can you justify making more than the president of the United States, Babe?" the writer asked.

Ruth's answer was simple and direct. "I had a better year."

I don't know if that conversation ever really took place or not, but it's a great story.

# CHAPTER 22

# Life in Washington

**I liked Dick Nixon.**

I know that's not a popular point of view and won't endear me to a lot of people, but the fact is, he was a very likable guy.

I first met Nixon when he was running for Vice President on Eisenhower's ticket, and I was convinced to join a group called "Athletes for Nixon."

In 1968, when he was campaigning for president against Hubert Humphrey, he came out to California often, and on many occasions, he and I would campaign in my district together. On those trips, he would also drag me along to campaign with him in the bay area for a few hours, then down to L.A. and San Diego. Nixon was a tireless campaigner and was a wizard at performing—and calling in—favors. From 1966, when he was defeated in the California gubernatorial election (when he told the press they wouldn't have Nixon to kick around any more) until he was nominated for the presidency in 1968, he traveled the country speaking at fund-raiser dinners and lunches for Republican senate and congressional candidates. Now it was time to call in those favors.

His Law and Order campaign turned out to be ironic when he became the first president to resign under a criminal cloud, but that was to come much later. The Nixon I knew was not the same Nixon who was hunkered down in the White House against the slings and arrows of Watergate.

My first term in Congress ended on the same day in January 1969 as did Lyndon Johnson's presidency. When Nixon became president, we lowly House Republicans were no longer *persona non grata* at the White House, and a feeling of euphoria was in the air.

We were now invited to lunches and receptions at the White House and were even allowed to enter through the front door!

During my second congressional term, I was selected to serve on the House Foreign Affairs Committee, and that gave me fairly frequent cause to hang around at the White House. I even got to travel on Air Force One once in a while.

People invariably ask me about this, the most famous airplane in the world, so I'll spend a paragraph or two on it. The most obvious and often-asked question is, what's it like?

First off, let me say that there is no single airplane actually designated as Air Force One. There are two planes, outfitted identically, that the president has at his disposal, and the one that he is on is always given that designation. If, say the vice president is traveling on government business and takes one of the two planes, that plane is often referred to as Air Force Two, but I believe that is an unofficial designation.

The aircraft itself is like the parable of the blind men trying to describe an elephant by feel.

Air Force One is different things to different people. Part of it is just like a passenger plane except the seating is all first class. Another part of the plane is divided into offices for the media and others who need to get work done.

Another part of it is, of course, the private quarters of the president.

I have no idea where they keep all the stuff, but I never once asked for anything while aboard Air Force One that wasn't available. It's the height of luxury, and, needless to say, security is tight as it always is when the president is present. I would imagine the maintenance given the plane is like no other vehicle in the world. They probably change the oil about every 100 miles.

Air Force One is in effect is a flying White House. It has all the efficiency of the White House, ready communications to anywhere in the world and just about anything you might need in the way of supplies if you were working. While you're on board you can call someone through the White House switchboard, and the party you're calling will hear: "This is the White House calling...." Tell me *that's* not impressive!

And yes, I confess, I stole matches and napkins from Air Force One. But that's nothing. I've seen people walk off the plane with dishes, antimacassars from the seat backs, notepads, glasses, hand towels, coffee mugs, even a large coffee urn. Anything that has the White House seal on it is fair game.

A state dinner at the White House is like no other experience in life.

We're told in grade school that one of the things that separates our country from Mother England is that we don't have a monarchy. Oh yeah? Attend just one state dinner at the White House, and then tell me we don't have a monarchy. These affairs are so rife with pomp and ceremony that you get to the point where you're afraid to eat. As a member of the House Foreign Affairs Committee, I was invited to many White House dinners, and each time was like the first time.

Tuxedos are usually required, and, of course the women wear evening gowns, and everyone is on their best behavior. My first impression was that there was a false sense of elegance, like at a college prom when we all dressed up formally and played at being adults, except this was the real thing. *This was elegance!*

If I was friendly with, say, Gerry Ford or Mel Laird—or Joe Blow—wouldn't you think it natural that we would sit together? Not a chance. You sat where you were told to sit. But at least you got to sit with your wife, right? Not a chance, again. Seating was carefully planned in advance, depending on the reason for the dinner, who the guests of honor were, which other guests were present, how much the president valued your presence at the time, and a lot of other details about which I didn't have a clue.

Each course is an adventure in good taste served by white-gloved waiters.

The person sitting next to you could be the ambassador from Nigeria, a Tory leader from Australia, the curator of the Smithsonian Institution, an astronaut, a rock star from Memphis, a scientist from M.I.T., or your next door neighbor from Virginia.

This was sure a far cry from dinner in Tulare when Eugene and I used to sling water at each other while we were supposed to be washing the dishes.

To enter the White House is to come face to face with living American history. Ironically, George Washington never made it to the White House, although he approved the design of the building and selected the site for it. John Adams, our second president moved in in November 1800 and was the first president to live in the mansion, but it still wasn't finished. Nor was it finished in March 1801 when Thomas Jefferson moved in.

Each President since has put his personal touches on the White House, so, in a way, you could say it still isn't finished.

There have been wings added, porches installed, offices moved, additional construction, and, of course, most new presidents redecorate the residential quarters and select their choice of furnishings for the Oval Office.

I had been to the White House but had not been in the Oval Office while Johnson was in office. I was in the Oval Office a number of times during Nixon's presidency and even more frequently once Gerry Ford took office.

But enough about the building; let's get back to Nixon—the man.

If ever there was a Washington insider, it was Richard Milhouse Nixon. Yet, paradoxically, from the first time I met him until he resigned the presidency, I had the feeling that *he* felt he didn't belong. It's been well documented that he trusted very few people, and there was always an aura of suspicion on his part. It's an understatement to say he wasn't a man of warmth, yet he was a man you wanted to be warm toward. The distance he kept made you feel almost as if he was on the outside looking in—yet he was the most powerful man in the world.

Like most young people growing up in the '30s and '40s, I had heard Franklin D. Roosevelt's fireside chats and could appreciate his gift for making Americans feel everything was going to be all right, even though the country was in chaos. In the '50s I listened to Adlai Stevenson's speeches and marveled at his command of the English language. A few years later, when I saw John Kennedy on television, I understood that he was the very embodiment of charisma.

Nixon was none of these. Nixon had none of FDR's avuncular tones, Stevenson's eloquence, nor Kennedy's grace and humor. And the interesting thing was, he knew it. I believe Nixon painted a very dark picture of himself, actually challenging you to like him.

I never could thoroughly sort out my feelings about Nixon other than that I found him likable in an unreachable sort of way. And when things started to go badly for him, he became even more unreachable. I was assigned to the Foreign Affairs Committee during Nixon's first term, and, whatever weaknesses Nixon's might have had, history has shown they weren't in foreign policy.

Because of my standing on two House committees, Agriculture and Foreign Affairs, I was asked to serve on the bipartisan International Food and Agriculture Organization. This was a group that got around. Our main mission was to impart as much American farming expertise to other parts of the world as possible. We often took farmers and other agricultural experts with us to other parts of the world so that they could examine and find ways to improve crop yield in other societies.

It never failed to amaze me how much we Americans took for granted, and farming was no exception. I had assumed that most of the equipment our farmers used was also in use around the world.

Nothing could have been farther from the truth. Some countries were unbelievably primitive in their farm techniques to the point where they were still using oxen—and in some cases—humans to pull their plows. Seeding was done by hand, and irrigation was either left to the rain gods or accomplished with buckets of water. The rotation of crops was a totally foreign concept to much of the world. When our farm experts explained how letting a field lie fallow for a season would enhance subsequent crops, they were met with a skepticism bordering on outright disbelief.

As my birthdays piled up, I experienced a strange metamorphosis. In the early days, after my athletic career ended, I just wanted to get on with my life, and it annoyed me sometimes when I would be introduced as Bob Mathias, the Olympic athlete. I would wonder to myself: "Won't I ever be anything but an Olympic athlete?" Now, in my 30s, I was just beginning to realize how special that Olympic experience was.

On one occasion, I was attending meetings in Germany at the Bundestag with other members of the Foreign Affairs Committee. When we were leaving with our West German counterparts, there was a group of teenagers outside the building. When they spotted us, they approached on the run with pads and pencils, indicating they were on the prowl for autographs.

I mentioned to one of the Germans that kids in his country treat politicians like celebrities, and he replied that it was *my* signature the kids were after. I remember thinking at the time that it was nice to not be forgotten.

My point is, if that had happened during my Olympic days, I would have thought nothing of it. But here, almost two decades after my last competition, I was just beginning to realize that I had done something that was still remembered, and it was nice. I suppose I had been an example of youth wasted on the young.

I still enjoy it when someone remembers me as an athlete or a congressman, and, while the days of adulation are far behind, it's just a nice feeling sometimes. It's kind of like getting a letter from an old friend.


Gerry Ford was one of my friends in the Congress, and he was one of the warmest, fairest most democratic men I ever met. I have always felt it was unfortunate he didn't have the opportunity to be president under different circumstances.

As minority leader of the House, he had a tremendous responsibility, that increased when Nixon took office.

It was one thing to have renegade Republican voters during a Democratic administration. A member of the Congress has the responsibility to vote his conscience on all issues regardless which party is in the White House. But when Nixon took over, Ford's job, as Minority Leader, was to deliver votes to Nixon. The reality was that Ford was in the position of having to deliver the votes or look incompetent as a leader.

Then the day came that the warm personal relationship Gerry Ford and I had built had to be put on hold.

All of a sudden, he was no longer Gerry, but rather, he became *Mr. President.*

In my second term in the House, I was beginning to feel less the tyro and more the old pro. After all, now there were freshmen congressmen asking *me* where the elevators were.

Midway through my second term, I participated in an exchange program between our government and that of France. A group of Deputies, which are the French equivalent of our congressmen, came to Washington to spend a few weeks in the U.S. Their first week would be spent in the Capitol, attending sessions and meetings with us and, in general, learning how our government functions.

We paired off in sort of a buddy system in which each deputy was assigned a Congressman to sort of shepherd him around Washington. I drew Jean Pierre Roux, the deputy from a district near Avignon, famous for its wines. Fortunately, Jean Pierre spoke fluent English because my ability to communicate in his language was limited to one year of college French.

Jean Pierre and I hit it off famously. He was intent on learning how our Congress functioned, and, since France also has a bicameral system, we had a commonality. The breakout of responsibilities within our three branches of government intrigued him because the French government is headed by a president and prime minister, who share the duties of governing. When I stated earlier that I believe in term limits, I could have mentioned as a bad example the French representative system. Their Deputies serve five-year terms, and their Senate members nine years.

The plan for the second week of the deputies' visit was for each of us Congressmen to take our deputy back to our district so he could get some flavor of the heartland of America—outside the beltway.

Well, now the story gets interesting.

It seems Jean Pierre had a colleague unto whom I shall affix the *nom faux* of Henri. Henri opted to go with us to California, rather than accompany his congressman to his district in Iowa.

My plan was for Jean Pierre, Henri and me to stay at my parents' house in Tulare, which we did at first. But after Henri realized how close we were to San Francisco, he insisted we go up there for a few nights as well. Who could blame him?

Once we got to San Francisco, we checked into the Fairmount Hotel, and that was the end of Henri.

We checked in at about three in the afternoon and went to our rooms. After a few minutes, I called Jean Pierre to see if he'd like to go to the bar for a drink. I suggested he call Henri as well. A few minutes after I arrived in the hotel bar, Jean Pierre came in—alone.

"Where's Henri?" I asked.

Jean Pierre smiled and shrugged.

Dinnertime came, and I suggested the Cafe Mozart two blocks away. Jean Pierre agreed, but when I suggested we get Henri, he smiled and shrugged.

After dinner, we sat in the lobby for awhile, and when it was time to go to bed, I asked Jean Pierre where Henri might be. He smiled and shrugged . . . again. The guy had simply disappeared, and after a while, I just stopped asking about him.

But I was fuming. Here I had taken this guy along with us as a favor and he pulled a major disappearing act without ever once saying a word. If it hadn't been for Jean Pierre's lack of concern, I would have been worried sick that the guy had been kidnapped or worse. Jean Pierre had reassured me a couple of times that he was okay and not to worry about him. So instead of being worried, I was just annoyed.

On the day we were to leave, Henri showed up in the lobby, his bags packed, ready to head back to D.C. without a word of explanation.

Once we arrived at the airport, I was able to get Jean Pierre aside and asked him, "Where the hell was your *ami* for four days?"

He smiled and, with an elaborate Gallic shrug, said simply: *"Cherchez la femme, Robair."*

The following year, as part of the same program, I visited Jean Pierre in Paris and his district, but the story ends there. We tended pretty much to business, and I never saw Henri the whole time we were there. Maybe he was cherchezing for femmes in his own backyard as well...

I talked earlier about all the goodies a Congressman has at his disposal. I never mentioned the other parts of Congressional life. The hours a conscientious congressman devotes to his job can be excruciatingly long for weeks on end. The travel is exhausting, and you can never—never—leave the job at the office. Then, every two years, you have to reapply for your job, and there is always stress in one form or another.

Melba and I seemed to be drifting away from each other through no fault of hers, nor of mine, I don't think. It wasn't as if we were battling with each other; we just didn't seem to have the closeness we once did. My job kept me away from home for days, sometimes weeks, at a time. And when I wasn't traveling, there were always issues dealing with the Congress, preparation for debates, position papers to be written, speeches to be prepared. Often, some of us would continue discussions on one matter or another, and the conversations often didn't end until midnight or beyond.

Meanwhile, Melba was stuck in the house raising the kids. We recognized it as a not-uncommon malady, given our lifestyle, and decided we wouldn't let it get the best of us. We planned a long vacation together, and when we came home, things seemed to be back to normal.

# CHAPTER *23*

# A Confession: Amateur Athlete Subsidies

**These were hellish times in America.** During my tenure in Congress, especially my second, third and fourth terms, the country—and for that matter, the world—was in almost constant upheaval.

Mr. Johnson's War in Southeast Asia was fast becoming Mr. Nixon's War, and the body bags were coming home in increasing numbers.

New African leaders were changing the face of the land, and that continent was awash in its own blood.

The Baader-Meinhof Gang was terrorizing West Germany as retribution for what it called U.S. Imperialism.

Within a period of weeks, Martin Luther King Jr. and Bobby Kennedy were assassinated.

The Arabs and Israelis were a constant threat to ignite the planet.

Charles Manson and his commune of sick hippies massacred actress Sharon Tate and four others.

American cities were engulfed in flames; 50,000 people gathered in front of the Lincoln Memorial to protest the Vietnam War.

And here we were, sitting in the nation's capital, wondering what the hell was going on.

On the other hand, not everything was going bad.

In July 1969, Buzz Aldrin and Michael Collins held their breath, and the rest of the world looked on as Neil Armstrong took a giant leap for mankind.

The Russians and the U.S. continued looking warily at each other but began the SALT talks aimed at reducing the rate of nuclear arms buildup.

Dr. Christiaan Barnard performed the world's first heart transplant, and Dr. Irving Cooper developed a treatment for Parkinson's disease through cryosurgery.

Color television became an affordable reality.

Sidney Poitier, Spencer Tracy and Katharine Hepburn teamed up in "Guess Who's Coming to Dinner?"

But on balance, times were pretty lousy.

The '60s were coming to an end, and I didn't know anyone who would mourn the decade.


As the decade was ending, new thoughts were stimulating me. I have a confession of sorts to make. Previously in this book I've complained about the present state of affairs in amateur athletics. As much as I hate to admit it, many of the problems I've complained about, especially about amateur athletes getting rich on training subsidies, is my own fault.

As 1969 was coming to a close, I was becoming more and more troubled about the state of amateur sports in America. In each Olympiad, we seemed to be losing more ground to the Eastern bloc countries. I knew it wasn't because our athletes were inferior, and I knew the Soviets had no secret weapons.

So, what was the problem?

On the surface, the problem was simple. It was a matter of training. The Soviets were doing a better job of training their athletes than we were. But beneath the surface, it was far more complex. It was actually a matter of societal philosophy.

Our athletes were amateurs in the strictest sense of the word. (Keep in mind we're talking about 1969.) Nothing significant had changed in the way our amateur athletes were treated since I had competed—since Jesse Owens had competed—since Jim Thorpe had competed.

Remember how they expunged Thorpe's records and took his medals away because he had been paid to play some baseball? Remember how I couldn't compete in 1956 because I had been paid to act in a movie about my life?

Amateur qualifications were unreasonable and inflexible. If you accepted money—even a single dollar—for anything related to your athletic ability—Bang! You were no longer an amateur, ergo, no Olympics for you, young man. It was a draconian system and was out of synch with the world of sports outside our national borders.

The Soviet system, on the other hand, was totally the opposite, and the word amateur had no meaning behind the Iron Curtain. Soviet bloc athletes were brought to special live-in camps where they were fed, trained and schooled in their specialty. They had training centers for swimmers, skaters, track and field, basketball, gymnastics, and most other Olympic sports.

It was a way of life behind the Iron Curtain. If a young Soviet was perceived to have exceptional ability in a particular sport, he became part of the system. The details of his life were taken care of by the state, and his *job* was to train and win an Olympic gold medal.

Compare that system to ours, where most of our athletes had to have full-time jobs and, in many cases, were supporting families. They trained when they could—at night, on weekends, after school, whenever. I knew how that worked, because I had been there.

The Iron Curtain countries understood that the way to put the best athlete on the field was to make training his or her number-one priority. The iron curtain athlete was, in effect, employed by the state.

We, on the other hand, were still living in the era of Frank Merriwell. Our philosophy hadn't changed from the early part of the century when gentleman athletes took the field of honor. Our hopelessly outdated notion of "For God, for Country, and for Yale" were still governing our amateur athletic program. We were still treating our Olympic athletes as if they were supported by family trust funds.

I was against subsidies as a matter of principle. On the other hand, I was also against getting our asses kicked in the Olympics. I thought there must be a middle ground somewhere and solicited opinions from Congressional colleagues as well as from the athletic community. While there was a great deal of support for subsidies, there was also the strong and widely held belief that a subsidized athlete is no longer an amateur athlete. It was becoming plain that, indeed, there might *not* be a middle ground.

The consensus was that a modified subsidy was like a slight case of pregnancy.

So, these opinions notwithstanding, I began thinking that the U.S. had to consider some kind of program that would assist amateur athletes in their training without completely compromising their amateur standing—to assist them, not support them.

An interesting sidelight was that the Russians were citing our college athletic scholarships and comparing them to *their* athletic subsidies.

One day, after conversations with my friends Bill Simon and Colonel Don Miller, I started making some notes to help me clarify my own thoughts on the subject. These notes became a position paper that eventually became the first draft of what I would some-day submit to the Congress as H.R. 11242: The Mathias Bill for Amateur Athlete Subsidy.

Revised versions of this bill would be incorporated into the Amateur Sports Act of 1978 and would eventually result in the development of the U.S. Olympic Training Center and training subsidies to amateur athletes.

I swear I had no idea that these subsidies would open the door to corporate sponsorship of athletes and get so out of control it would result in millionaire *amateur* athletes.

### President Gerald R. Ford:

*There was a long-standing feud between the Amateur Athletic Union (AAU) and the National Collegiate Athletic Association (NCAA), and they continually fought back and forth about who had the right to represent the U.S. athletes in the Olympics. It was a real mess.*

*I appointed Jerry Sarno, the former head of Eastman Kodak, to lead a group to try to resolve the conflict. They came up with a recommendation that a compromise be put into effect between the AAU and the NCAA. To implement that, we needed the type of legislation that Bob Mathias sponsored.*

*The result of that bill (and the legislation that ultimately passed) was that it ended the personal feuds and territoriality between the AAU and the NCAA and set up the U.S. Olympic Committee as the governing body for Olympic athletes. We ended up with far better representation in the Olympics.*

*After 20 years, I can look back and see that it wasn't perfect, but I still think it was good legislation. In some respects, perhaps we undercut the bona fide amateur label, but if you're going to compete, you should have the right to play by the same rules as everybody else does.*


While I was fretting about the state of amateur athleticism in the country, there were other things going on in Washington.

On a Saturday morning in June 1972, a reporter who had been employed by the *Washington Post* for only nine months answered the phone at his apartment in downtown Washington. His name was Bob Woodward.

# CHAPTER 24

# Watergate!

**The world of politics,** the world of reporting and the very government itself was about to undergo sea changes.

I was there. I was there for Nixon's 1968 campaign against Hubert Humphrey and his 1972 campaign against George McGovern. I was there when Senator Thomas Eagleton was forced to resign from the '72 Democratic ticket because he had been treated for supposed mental illness; when Vice President Spiro Agnew was forced to resign his office in 1973.

And I was there when the President of the United States resigned to avoid being impeached.

Looking back, it's a tribute to the U.S. Constitution that the republic survived the crises of the '60s and '70s. I don't think any other government, with the possible exception of Great Britain, could have.

If you'd like to read one of the great political books of all-time—one that pulls no punches, is as objective as a book on politics can be and tells it like it is (or was) throughout—I highly recommend Theodore H. White's *The Making of the President, 1972.* It is the fourth and final book in White's series chronicling presidential elections beginning with the Kennedy-Nixon campaign in 1960. The book shows extreme insight and perception in that much of what we learned about Watergate didn't come out until after the book was published. Therefore, White's reportage is done without the benefit of hindsight.

In my opinion—which was shared by many at the time—the Watergate incident was one of the most preventable tragedies in American history. Reporters have written of "the inevitable downhill spiraling of trust and faith in the Nixon administration."

Hell, there was nothing inevitable about it. These guys were compounding their own problems each day. At any point over the first six or eight months, if someone had just said, "Yeah, we did it. It was stupid and inexcusable, and we're sorry," Watergate would have gone away. After a while, of course, it was too late. There had been too many lies from too many people who shouldn't have been lying.

I have searched my memory for my reactions, but it's difficult to say for sure what I actually remember from firsthand exposure, and what I *think* I remember but *might* have read in the paper. I do remember that when Watergate first broke, I had conversations with colleagues from both sides of the aisle, and the general feeling was that Ben Bradlee (executive editor) and Katharine Graham (the publisher of the *Washington Post*) had their knives out for the president.

We Republicans were mostly annoyed at the coverage of such a minor thing, and the Democrats, for the most part, were amused, but no one ever dreamed how far the shame would eventually travel.

I believed John Mitchell and Maurice Stans when, in the very beginning, they denied any wrongdoing.

I believed H.R. Haldeman and John Ehrlichmann later on.

I thought John Dean was out to get them all.

I certainly believed Nixon without any hesitation when, early on, he said: "The White House has had no involvement whatever in this particular incident. "

"*Finally, a denial. Now it's over,*" I thought then. I wasn't nearly as astute or as suspicious as Bob Woodward and Carl Bernstein in their skepticism of the phrase . . . "this particular incident. "

In a way, it *was* over then. Over for Nixon. But, of course, nobody would know that for two more years.

It's a pity that such an ultimately inconsequential act could have thrown the country into such cataclysmic turmoil for so long. From the middle of the summer of 1972 through August 1974, when Nixon finally resigned—that's more than two years—the country was obsessed by Watergate. And the incident itself was nothing more than stupid. It was the lying and the deceit and the snowballing cover-ups that got everyone in trouble.

When I was a kid, my mother told me never to lie because when you lie two things happen: First, you have to remember what you said. Second, you have to keep lying to cover up your first lie.

Was she smart or what?


Most of us in the House and the Senate tried to get on with our lives and the business of governing the country despite the cyclone swirling around the capitol. Even though I, and most of my congressional colleagues, were always at arms length from the White House, it still was difficult to function and impossible to ignore.

At first, there was just an occasional article in the *Washington Post,* but as the stories continued and were given more space and began to draw in more and more people, I remember feeling at first, that Bob Woodward and Carl Bernstein were just two young reporters trying to make a name for themselves. Then, after many months, I began thinking that some of my friends might actually be involved in this thing.

In retrospect, I have to admire the reporting of Woodward and Bernstein when I compare it to the irresponsible sensationalism, which is the hallmark of today's media. Woodward and Bernstein's interest was in pursuing their story, and they weren't looking for gossip or juicy sidebars. Today's reporters seem far more intent on *asserting* than *confirming*.

The story continued to develop, and pretty soon the *New York Times* checked in.

Then, when it really got to be hot stuff, it seemed that reporters from every newspaper, magazine, TV and radio station in the country —*in the world, perhaps*—were standing there with a pad or a microphone when you ventured out of your office or the House chamber. Many of these guys would have interviewed a penguin if they could find one that could talk.

They didn't much care who you were or what you knew. They were breathlessly on the prowl for anything and anyone who would give them a quote. "Congressman Mathias, Congressman Mathias, how did *you* feel when you learned that all your private conversations in the Oval Office were taped?"

I'd never had a private conversation in the Oval Office, but some of these people were so pitiable in their thirst for a quote that after a while, there was a temptation to give them something.

"Well, Jed," I'd think to myself, "at breakfast just this morning, the president confided to me he was adding video cameras and blood pressure machines in the oval office. That way, he'll be able to record the emotions of people he is speaking with. But, of course, that's off the record, Jed."

I could see the next day's headlines:

UNNAMED CONGRESSMAN CONFIRMS
PRESIDENT SUFFERING FROM PARANOIA


It's been well documented how meticulously the *Post* and its editors demanded confirmed sources from Woodward and Bernstein throughout their reportage of Watergate. It's frightening to think what turmoil the country might have been thrown into if the reportorial standards of that day had sunk to the lows of the media covering President Clinton's Whitewater affair, Travelgate, Monica Lewinsky and the lurid, unconfirmed reporting that's pandemic today.


When it comes down to it, with a few exceptions, we in the Congress were just like our constituents back home. Most of what we knew we learned from the *Washington Post.*

The fact is, Watergate never had a thing to do with the Republican Party, although we Republicans took the brunt of the blame and criticism. The entire operation had been staged and covered up by the Committee to Reelect the President—aptly nicknamed CREEP.

Over the years many people have asked me: "Did I believe the president?"

Of course I did. He was the president of the United States for God's sake. I believed him for a long time, and I believed his denials. I never quite trusted some of the people he kept around him, but the president was the president, and I believed him. I think, looking back over the experience, part of the reason I believed him was because I wanted to.

Shortly after being sworn in for my fourth term in Congress, in January 1973, I went back home to tend to some business in the district. I was amazed at the impact Watergate was having on the country in general. Needless to say, Capitol Hill had been consumed by the scandal, but I was surprised to see the frenzy of concern in the general public. I guess I shouldn't have been. After all, with television as the medium of communication, news got to California just as quickly as it got to the floor of the House.

However, the pressure in the district to do something was tremendous. I had been pretty much on the fence on the issue, only slowly realizing its true depth and breadth. But because of each new revelation disclosing new facts and new names, I was beginning to lean toward abandoning Nixon. I was convinced, as, it seems was the whole country, that there had been plenty of wrongdoing.

I had always felt the stance Nixon had taken was not so much to cover himself as it was to protect those who worked for him.

But when I visited my district and learned just how strong the sentiment against him was, I couldn't possibly justify any further support. If I was to represent the wishes of my constituency, which was my sworn responsibility, I had to declare against the president; not an easy thing to do for someone who had been brought up to respect the office without exception.

As the Watergate issue ground on, I found myself becoming closer and closer to Gerry Ford–not ever suspecting what might be in store for him.

Then, in 1973, when Spiro Agnew was forced to resign and Nixon appointed Gerry vice president, I was stunned. Elated but stunned. Here was a guy who was my friend. He was Gerry, and I was Bob.

Now he was going to be vice president of the United States.

I never got to know Agnew well, but I knew Gerry Ford was an honest and honorable man. He was respected in the House, was the epitome of decency, and I knew he would make a great vice president. When I gave him my heartfelt congratulations, he gave me a shrug as if he had a thought he wasn't expressing.

And so he did. Little did we know it at the time, but it wouldn't be long before they were they were to begin the process of "throwing the rascals out."

There was an awkward time immediately after the Nixon resignation. In my first meeting with now President Ford, he asked me a question, and I had to catch myself. I was about to say something like: "The way I see it, Gerry . . . ."

But Gerry was no longer Gerry. He was now Mr. President

It was a weird feeling. Here was a man who had been my mentor and good friend, yet custom forbade me from addressing him in the manner I had for years. I remember him saying to me: "Nothing has changed Bob, just my job."

Yeah, right, you're only the President of the United States now. Other than that, nothing has changed.


Anyone who lived through that period in American history who didn't become absolutely enamored with the U.S. Constitution didn't realize what we had gone through and just what an incredibly strong, unique and adaptable document it is.

# CHAPTER 25

# AAU vs. NCAA!

**I realize, compared to Watergate,** the subject of amateur athletics pales. However, despite the turmoil, life—and legislation—had to go on.

Because I was convinced that we had to compete on a level playing field with the Iron Curtain countries, I continued developing my athletics bill for the Congress to review and, hopefully, to act on.

By 1972, the constant feuding between the NCAA and the AAU was reaching critical mass, and our amateur athletes were being whipsawed by the two factions.

I'm grateful to my friend Mike Harrigan, a White House aide at the time, who was able to refresh my memory and provide me with a long-lost document regarding many of the events that eventually led to the Amateur Sports Act of 1978. To best reflect the attitude of the times, I have taken parts of the following from the "History and Current Status of Amateur Sports Problems in the United States," a document written by Mike and published in August 1975 for the President's Commission on Olympic Sports.

In some cases, I will paraphrase that document, and in others, I will quote it directly. For the sake of clarity, I do not make a distinction.

To understand the problem, we first have to look at the mechanics of international competition as they had been prior to 1978.

Let's hypothetically suppose the U.S. and the Soviet Union wanted to participate in a track meet against each other. This meet, like any other amateur competition, would have to be approved by the world sports federation for that sport. That federation is made up of affiliates from each country that participates internationally in track and field. The federation would have to approve the meet, but the details would be worked out between the affiliates of the countries involved.

In the U.S., the affiliate was the Amateur Athletic Union (AAU), which was recognized as the governing body for international "open" track and field competition.

Now that term "open."

Let's say Stanford and Cal (UC-Berkeley) go against each other in a track meet. That meet would be considered restricted rather than open, because it is not open to participants outside those two universities. Likewise, a PAC-10 track meet would be considered restricted for the same reason. The intercollegiate athletic activities of Stanford and Cal, as well as the PAC-10, are governed by the National Collegiate Athletic Association (NCAA).

Now, let's go back to the track meet between the U.S. and the U.S.S.R. This would be considered an "open" event, and, as such would be sanctioned by the AAU. However, let's say the participants were a mix of college athletes, military personnel and some who never went to college.

Who would have jurisdiction? The AAU or the NCAA?

The AAU's position would be that because it was an open meet, *it* would have jurisdiction. The NCAA's position would be that since there were college athletes involved—and the NCAA was sworn to protect them from worldly evils—the meet would be under *its* jurisdiction.

To compound the situation, since the track season is a finite one, the U.S./U.S.S.R. meet would conflict with a number of college meets. This would further strengthen (in the NCAA's mind) the case for *it* being the controlling body for this meet.

Now the AAU would have come back and pointed out that *it* was the only body recognized by the world federation, therefore, the NCAA would not be entitled to any jurisdiction—*nor to any of the revenue generated by the meet!*

Surprise, surprise. It all comes down to dollars!

I presented the above as a hypothetical, but it was happening all the time. Because of the decentralized power and its abuses, there were three conclusions that could be drawn:

1.) Sports bodies were known to manipulate their athletes as puppets when it suited their purposes, not considering the athletes to have any rights whatsoever.

2.) Objectives in building prestige and international understanding were damaged because often the team that took the field was less than the best collection of athletes available.

3.) The potential talent of U.S. athletes was going unrealized at all stages of development, because the various governing bodies were so preoccupied with their intramural battles that they had lost sight of their overall objective—to put the best team possible on the field.

Keeping in mind my hypothetical, here is an *actual* example of how this squabbling affected our on-the-field performance.

In March 1973, the U.S.S.R. national track and field team came to Richmond, Virginia, to compete against the U.S. national team in an indoor meeting. American athletes had been selected for the competition by way of the national track and field championships. As in the hypothetical case, the athletes who had qualified came from many jurisdictions, one of which was the NCAA. Because this meeting with the Russians was international and an open competition, it was sanctioned and conducted by the AAU.

The NCAA demanded more of a voice in conducting the tournament. The AAU declined. The NCAA then ordered the athletes under its jurisdiction (all those currently attending college) not to compete.

The United States lost the meet.

There is little question that if the NCAA-governed athletes had been allowed to take part, the United States would have won. Despite the NCAA ban, two NCAA athletes chose to defy the organization and compete. When they did, court action was taken against them.

Although the cases were subsequently dropped, it should be pointed out that *two American athletes had faced possible prosecution for their desire to represent their country in competition against the Soviet Union.*

What's more, neither of the athletes had academic schedule conflicts or other tournament commitments at their schools that would have precluded them from competing.

There were uncountable incidents like this—some more devastating to our national sports psyche than others—but all counterproductive to us as a nation wanting to show our athletic ability in international competition.

The NCAA/AAU conflict was not the only organizational problem. There were also military athletic programs, the National Association of Intercollegiate Athletics (NAIA: the governing body for smaller colleges) and other jurisdictional fiefdoms.


There was a crying need for centralized jurisdiction, and many of my congressional colleagues saw me, as a former Olympian, the logical choice to work on a bill that might alleviate the problem. I certainly needed no urging.

What was needed was:

1.  A comprehensive analysis of the organizations controlling amateur sports and their interconnected roles.
2.  Specific recommendations on changes that should be made to eliminate jurisdictional disputes.
3.  A mandate to determine what should be the proper stance of the federal government in its relationship to the world of amateur sports.

My proposed legislation, known romantically as H.R.11242 was the first of a number of bills submitted to Congress to provide a uniform training program for amateur athletes. It was not passed—nor were many subsequent bills—but each succeeding bill built on the strengths of the previous ones until there was, finally, legislation that Congress could live with.

### Mike Harrigan, former White House aide:

*While the ultimate Amateur Sports Act borrowed concep-tually from some of the earlier proposals, the ultimate Act was far superior to anything that had been proposed previously. Most important, it was successfully passed when all other previous efforts had not come close to full passage. Ironically, and as I predicted at the time, the most egregious "sticking point" to get-ting the ultimate ASA passed was not the act itself but rather the one-time authorization of federal money that was attached to it.*

*Politicians of all stripes objected to the use of federal money for amateur sports, and it added an undesirable, unrelated di-mension to an already delicate compromise within and among sports groups.*

Mike points out an amusing sidebar to the issue.

Liberals didn't object to giving federal money to amateur sports but didn't care about beating the Russians. Conservatives wanted to beat the Russians but were very circumspect regarding federal money for amateur sports because of the federal control it might bring.

While I don't intend to include the text of H.R. 11242 in this book, I will point out that it is available to the general public—and especially those suffering from insomnia—at the Library of Congress.

Here are some of Mike Harrigan's comments about the Mathias Bill:

*"The principal elements of H.R. 11242 were its provi-sions for compulsory, binding arbitration by the American Ar-bitration Association of challenges to sports organizations which*

*purported to represent the United States internationally. The Arbitration Association also would have settled claims by athletes, coaches, trainers, etc., that they had been denied the right to qualify for, or participate in, international sports competition. The bill would have been an amendment of the Olympic Charter.*

*"The Mathias bill went a long way toward providing a set of rights for amateur athletes as well as for others involved in amateur sports. In fact, the NCAA and some other school-oriented groups charged that the bill went too far.*

*"These groups maintained that the athletes' rights provisions contained in H.R.11242 were so strong, that many college, conference, and high school athletic procedures designed to protect the educational institutions from unregulated outside competition or recruiting abuses would have become unenforceable. Additionally, these school-college groups pointed out that because of certain threshold requirements, there would have been some doubt about the effectiveness of the provisions that were designed to protect the athlete from unfair rulings of the sports-governing bodies.*

*"The Cook-Humphrey amendment was a rewritten and strengthened version of the Mathias Bill. It was offered as a substitute to the Amateur Sports board approach in S. 3500 during the senate floor debate on the measure. The amendment contained not only a fairer, more balanced procedure for effecting change in sports governing bodies but also a set of strong and specific steps to be taken to help assure that a turnover in power, in fact, would be made as the result of a successful challenge through arbitration."*

My bill was followed by H.R. 7918, the O'Hara Bill, then S. 1018, which was sponsored by Senator John Tunney. The Tunney Bill proposed that a commission be established to review the participation of the United States in the Olympic games.

There was no shortage of attention to the matter. Jack Kemp also sponsored a bill, H.R. 15241, which represented an attempt to correct the direction and scope of the commission that was proposed in the Tunney Bill. Using the same framework, Jack's bill also proposed a national commission be appointed to recommend solutions to these problems.

The fact that I was so heavily involved in trying to make sure our Olympic athletes had a good training facility to pursue their Olympic goals would create an irony a few years after I left the Congress.

But—again—I'm getting ahead of myself.

# CHAPTER 26

*In the early eighteenth century, Alexander Pope wrote his* Farewell to London. *His opening line seems a fitting title for this chapter.*

# "Dear, Damn'd Distracting Town, Farewell"

**A good part of my fourth term** was given over to the development of legislation to assist our amateur athletes. We Republicans also spent a great deal of time dodging bullets aimed at the Committee to Reelect the President and the Watergate people.

We couldn't know at the time what impact Watergate was going to have on Republicans in the 1974 Congressional elections, so most of us just tried to do our jobs and cope as best we could with the political environment. And let the chips fall where they may.

But it was safe to assume it wouldn't be good.

We thought perhaps when Nixon resigned and Ford moved into the Oval Office, it would end the fallout, but there was just too much bitterness in the country.

In the spring of 1974, we began preparing for the November race.

As I looked over the field of possible opponents, in the back of my mind was always the thought that Watergate was not doing me any good. The fact that Spiro Agnew had come to Bakersfield for a fund-raiser early in that term, before his forced retirement, hadn't helped me a great deal either.

In traveling my district earlier in the year, I could feel the vitriol aimed at Nixon. Not only was Nixon a target but his entire administration as well and, in general, the Republican Party.

I had always had such a great, open relationship with my constituents and there had always been a lot of give and take in our meetings. Now, when I went back to the district, I noticed a hesitancy to speak; almost a sense that the voters had something they wanted to tell me but were too embarrassed to say. The contrast with past meetings was sobering.

The fact that my district was 60 percent Democratic had never been a factor, so I wasn't worried about that. I was, however, concerned about the changing logistics and demographics of the district.

Each election year, liberal Congressman Phil Burton from the San Francisco bay area did a little finagling with the layout of the district, trying to overbalance the Democratic voting base. Phil's brother, John, now the leader of the Democratically controlled State Senate in Sacramento, was then an Assemblyman, which enabled Phil to chip away at the boundaries of my 18th District. While I always considered Phil a friend, it's true what they say about politicians being strange bedfellows.

In 1974, Phil and the Democratic-controlled state legislature succeeded in getting the 18th District lines redrawn to include Fresno—a huge concentration of longtime Democrats, union workers and minorities which translated to a lot of votes against Mathias.

But in the words of *MAD* Magazine's Alfred E. Newman— "What, Me Worry?" I had represented my district well and fairly for almost eight years and was confident the voters would return me to office.

My opponent, John Krebs, was Chairman of the Board of Supervisors of Fresno County and, because of his local affiliations, had an excellent base of support.

I knew I would be in for a tough fight, but that never bothered me. In fact, I always felt I functioned better when I had obstacles in front of me. But there was one particular obstacle I didn't anticipate: COPE.

COPE is the Committee on Political Education, the political action arm of the AFL-CIO, and it had targeted California's 18th District for a Democratic victory.

I felt the influence of COPE in my first debate with Krebs.

It took place in Hanford, a small town in Kings County. I knew from past experience that an incumbent's voting record always comes into question (that was one of the ways I won my first term), so I had a folder with me that contained my voting record and a few other salient facts about the past term.

John Krebs showed up with a huge—I mean huge—book, bound in black and bearing the COPE emblem on the front cover. The debate went along for awhile, John challenging some of my votes, mentioning that I had only met 85% of the votes and quorum calls and some other stuff that I had anticipated. We debated back and forth on issues such as Medicare, Social Security, foreign affairs and the usual issues. As is usually the case, the challenger challenges and the incumbent defends.

I responded, defending my voting record, pointing out that an 85% voting record was above average and thought I was holding my own pretty well. The issue of Watergate kept coming up, and I kept deflecting it, saying *I* was not responsible for the scandal nor was the Republican Party. It had been the actions of a handful of misguided people working for CREEP.

Then, toward the end of the allotted time, some guy stands up and asks Krebs: "How would you have voted on the D.C. Limousine Issue?"

"Uh oh," I thought. "What is this?"

I didn't even know what the question was about. What the hell was the D.C. Limousine Issue?

Mr. Krebs pronounced the D.C. Limousine Issue almost as big a scandal as Watergate. Then he turned to me and said: "But you, Mr. Mathias, voted in favor of these limousines, spending taxpayers' money for the privileged few."

I couldn't even defend myself, because I still had no idea what he was talking about, and it was obvious. Finally, I said the only thing I could think of. I said: "Could you be more specific?"

He plunged right into his big black book and miraculously found the page he was looking for immediately. He read the name of a bill that had been passed by the House the previous year. Now I remembered. The bill had been more than four-inches thick, and somewhere within the hundreds of thousands of words, it authorized chauffeur-driven cars for certain cabinet members and other high-ranking officials.

I pointed out that the bill had been passed almost unanimously by the House, and that the cars weren't for pleasure, they were to make travel around the capital more convenient and efficient for some people whose time was at a premium.

But it was too late. The damage had been done. Not only did I look like a dunce when the question came up, my response had been lame and weak.

The limousine issue became a campaign theme for Krebs, and the very next morning there was a 30- second TV commercial on the morning news featuring John Krebs talking about "Mr. Mathias' support for all the big limousine people in Washington." Obviously, the spot had been produced with the help of the COPE people weeks before.

A few weeks later, I learned that Krebs had been driving a taxpayer-paid car for years, but when I brought it up as an issue, it came across as petty, as well as being too late.

Another issue that Krebs exploited was the Absentee Theme. He ran a commercial showing a big empty chair, and a voice-over talked about Bob Mathias' pathetic voting record and the fact that I had missed almost 15% of all votes. I can't imagine a Congressman with a 100% voting record. That would mean that he was always in Washington, never in his district doing the work of his constituents. As I said earlier, mine was a better than average record, but the point was that the commercial put me on the defensive.

A major fallout of Watergate was the fact that political contributions had dried up considerably. I had a tough time raising money for my campaign. In the past, it had been just a matter of making a few phone calls; the people I called would call others, they would call others and the checks would start coming in. This wasn't happening in 1974.

The little money we had for the campaign had to be husbanded, and so we decided to delay going on television until the latter stages of the campaign. Unfortunately, by the time we had the funds available, most of the good commercial TV time slots had been filled.

Believe it or not, with all this going against me, I was still optimistic about winning. And I think I might have if it hadn't been for the apathy within Republican voter ranks. That was what finally nailed me. It wasn't until after the election was over that I learned what had happened to my voting base.

It seemed the Republican voters decided they couldn't support their party in this election because of Watergate.

Yet they would never vote Democrat, so they just didn't vote. The local Republican machine didn't mount a "Get Out the Vote" campaign as they always had done in the past, and that was that.

The final vote count was 51% to 49% in favor of John Krebs. I believe that if the normal number of Republicans—who usually vote—had voted, I would have won another term.

I did not deal particularly well with losing.

When Krebs was projected as the winner around midnight, I was in a hotel in Fresno. I sent John a note congratulating him and then headed down to my campaign headquarters and thanked all my volunteers.

There was a request for me to appear on an election wrap-up show at a local TV studio, so I headed over there. But about halfway there, I decided I didn't want some guy with beautiful hair and a great smile sticking a microphone in my face and saying: "Gee Bob, it doesn't look good for you does it?" Nor was I anxious to answer probing questions like: "How does it feel to lose?"

So I just said the hell with it and told my driver to head back to the hotel. Not very gracious, but as I thought back on the incident, I realized I'd had very little experience with losing, and I just didn't like it. As a team member, my football and basketball teams had lost very few games—maybe two or three a year at most...in both sports combined. I had never lost a decathlon and had never lost an election up until that night.

My feelings were somewhere between disappointed, pissed off, and wondering what the hell had happened.

It was small solace that I wasn't alone.

Fifty-seven Republicans had been defeated that night, the largest number of incumbents to lose an election until President Clinton's midterm election in 1994, when 63 House Democrats were beaten.

On the other hand, I had always thought of my job in Congress as a two-year job, so it wasn't particularly difficult to accept my loss. It was the actual act of losing that I had trouble coming to grips with. If that sounds contradictory, it's because I had contradictory thoughts at the time. In retrospect, if I had been more aggressive, I might have won, but—also in retrospect—I believe I was in Congress long enough. I was there for eight years; accomplished as much as I probably would have in 28 years, and it was time to turn the job over to a new man.

I just didn't like losing.

# CHAPTER 27

## Life Goes On

**The obvious question, "What now?"** was answered a week or so later.

I had been dreading the thought of packing up the house and moving. Not that Washington was such a great place, but moving had become, in my mind, a symbol of defeat.

One day, I answered the phone, and the voice on the other end said: "The White House is calling."

President Ford's office was on the phone to ask me if I would consider the position of Deputy Director of the Selective Service System.

It wasn't exactly what I'd been trained for, but on the other hand, it *was* a paycheck.

So, when my Congressional term ended in January 1975, I took about six months off and in June reported to work at the Selective Service offices.

On my first day, I was introduced around, shown my office— a huge office—sat behind my desk—a huge desk—ready to tackle the problems of the world.

And I sat.

And sat.

And sat.

About a week later, I was asked to visit the Director. If I thought *my* office was big, his was the size of a small town. He asked me how it was going, and I told him, frankly, I was bored as hell.

"Why don't you spend some time touring the Regional Offices?" he suggested.

"Fine," I thought. "Anything's better than sitting here with nothing to do."

So I went on tour, visiting selective service offices around the country. Instead of sitting around *my* office doing nothing, now I got to sit around *other people's* offices doing nothing.

I was able to take this for only two months and had already written my letter of resignation when, thankfully, another message came from the White House.

Would I be interested in working on President Ford's 1976 campaign finance committee?

Would I?

I'd have been interested in judging a beautiful owl contest if it would get me out of the Selective Service job.

This position, too, was to prove temporary. But short though it was, it proved very satisfying.

It was a fascinating four-and-a-half months, from mid-August through the end of December 1975, in which I got to meet and work with David Packard (yes, that's as in Hewlett-Packard) who was the National Chairman of President Ford's Campaign Finance Committee.

Packard was a wonderful and highly intelligent man to work for, and, after meeting him, it was easy to see how he had become so successful.

Our committee was charged with raising the necessary funding for President Ford to run his election campaign.

I wasn't particularly knowledgeable about fund-raising, and, in fact, it was the aspect about running for election that I enjoyed the least. I found it very difficult to ask people for money, so you might think I was ill-suited for this position.

On the contrary, it was a good match. I wasn't going to be asking for money. They had professionals doing that. I was an organizer, administrator, and liaison agent.

Those were the very early days of laws governing campaign financing. Congress had passed rules and regulations that were brand new and that needed explanation and interpreting, and it would be my responsibility to provide that information and education to state and local Republican Party chairmen.

Once again, I was on the road almost continually, putting a further strain on my marriage, but I told myself at the time that it was a job that had to be done.

The preparation for each trip was pretty intense, because we were dealing with a heretofore unknown factor. Up until this time, there had been no rules governing how a candidate could raise money: Special interest groups and businesses with legislative interests could contribute as much as they wanted to any candidate who they had reason to believe would champion their cause in Congress.

If you think present-day campaign fund-raising is a mess, I assure you it was a lot worse when we first enacted rules governing it. It just didn't get the media attention it gets today.

Anyway, the Mathias Traveling Circus and Finance Information Program got underway in the fall of 1975, and I hit something like 23 states in 75 days.

I remember most clearly the time I spent with the Texas Republican Committee.

I flew in to Dallas on Monday and spent the day with Trammel Crowe, a wealthy developer and chairman of the Texas Republican Party Finance Committee. I briefed him on the information we had to get across to his local finance chair people and gave him copies of the literature that had been prepared as leave-behinds.

Trammel then took me on his private plane to meetings throughout the state for training sessions with the local finance people. Needless to say, not all state chairmen had their own planes, but in Texas, private planes aren't at all uncommon among people of Crowe's means.

Trammel spoke to the group, stating the purpose of our visit, then introduced me with a flourish, acknowledging that, yes, I was *that* Bob Mathias. Then I got down to explaining the new finance rules. There were a lot of questions, and I was pleased (not to mention a little surprised) that I had most of the answers. Occasionally, though, I'd get stuck. For instance, one question in particular really threw me.

I had finished my presentation in a meeting room at a local Holiday Inn and was in the process of passing out the literature that summarized what we had just discussed. One man, who had been intensely reading a pamphlet, looked up and raised his hand.

"Do you have a question?" I asked him.

"Yeh, how does this work?"

I thought I had heard all the questions by that time, but here was a new one. "How does *what* work?" I responded.

"This finance stuff."

I had no idea what he was talking about. We had just spent over an hour on *this finance stuff.*

"What aspect of it don't you understand?" I asked.

"The part about raising the money."

Now there was a little snickering in the room. I asked him: "Could you be a little more specific?"

"Why would the publicity committee be involved in raising money?" After asking his question, he looked around at the surprised smiles in the room and got this confused look on his face. "Or...isn't this the publicity committee?" He finished lamely.

Someone in the audience gently told him the publicity committee was holding an organizational meeting in another room in the same hotel. The poor guy had spent over an hour in a dry financial meeting when he could have been enjoying himself in a room full of publicists.


As I said earlier, this position was to be short-term, which was fortunate, because my personal life was in turmoil.

Melba and I had drifted so far apart that there wasn't much point in our continuing to live together. We separated in early 1976. I stayed in Washington, and Melba took the kids back to California to live.

It was just an awful time for me, for Melba and certainly for the kids. I remember thinking to myself once: "If I were a drinking man, these would be good times to drink." It would have been easy to feel sorry for myself, and, I guess to some degree I did, but I knew better times were ahead. I didn't know where or how, but all my life I was able to turn bad times around.

But at this particular time, my feelings were mainly of guilt and shame. Guilt that it was my life and job that had taken me away from Melba and the kids in the first place and shame in that no one in my family had ever been divorced before. And it was obvious that Melba and I were headed in that direction.

It was the fall of 1976 when the wheels really came off the wagon.

In October, Melba and I agreed that it was pointless to try to keep the marriage together, so we started taking the necessary steps toward divorce. So, my personal life was a shambles. I had seen it coming but was always too involved in my public life and my career to face it realistically. But now, it was a reality and it was upon me.

And in November, President Ford lost the election to Jimmy Carter.

Earlier that year, Ford had asked me to serve on the President's Council on Physical Fitness, which I was glad to do, but now there didn't seem to be much point. He would no longer be president, and chances were that Carter would want to bring in his own people. So I left my position and moved back to California.

Alone.

And unemployed.

It was time to regroup.

# CHAPTER 28

# A New Beginning

**Before I had resigned from the President's Council,** I had been doing a great deal of traveling and speechmaking for the Council as well as for a number of private groups. These travels had taken me to Memphis a couple of times, and, one night in a hotel room, I was looking at a road map in order to plan my next day's travels, and I noticed I wasn't far from Forrest City, Arkansas.

In my early days on Capitol Hill, I had become acquainted with Bill Alexander, a Democratic Congressman from Arkansas. Bill and his wife Gwen, and Melba and I had attended many embassy parties and social functions.

I had been impressed with Gwen the very first time I had met her. She was not only a beautiful woman, but she had a personality and wit to match. We had gotten along great on those occasions when we were together with our spouses, and I saw no reason why we shouldn't still be compatible. I knew that Bill and Gwen had also divorced, and that Gwen was living in her hometown of Forrest City.

I was not thinking of a permanent relationship when I got her number from the long-distance operator and called her. When she twanged her hello, I identified myself, and it was like the years between had vanished. We gabbed for over an hour that first night, and I agreed I would try to get to Forrest City before I left for home.

We had what would be described in a romance novel as a whirlwind courtship, even though she was in Arkansas and I was in California. I began looking for speaking engagements in that part of the country and sometimes would drive two or three hours to see Gwen after my business was finished.

As happy as we were when we were able to get together, there was this little problem. My divorce still hadn't been finalized, so I was relieved (from a legal point of view) on December 7, 1977, when I received an official-looking document telling me Melba and I were no longer married.

I must say I had really conflicting feelings about the finalization of my divorce. On the one hand, it made me look back with a lot of regret on where we had gone wrong, and, of course, I was always concerned about the well-being of the kids. On the other hand, now I was free to pursue a relationship with Gwen. We didn't waste any time, and on New Year's Eve, Gwen and I were married.

I will deny to my dying day that I was motivated by a tax deduction.

# CHAPTER *29*

# The U.S. Olympic Training Center

**So here I was, newly married—and newly employed.**

The 1976 Olympics in Montreal were well run games in which my friend Bruce Jenner had a great victory in the decathlon. However, the U.S. team overall didn't perform up to expectations, and the U.S. Olympic Committee people began asking themselves what they could do to help American Olympians do better in international competition.

The answer they came up with was to implement an Olympic training center, and they chose California's magnificent Squaw Valley, site of the 1960 Winter Games. The facility already had dorms and a dining room as well as skiing and ice skating accommodations.

Early in 1977, shortly after I had left the President's Council on Physical Fitness, I was in touch with a friend from my Washington days: Colonel F. Don Miller. Don had been head of the Modern Pentathlon National Governing Body. The Modern Pentathlon had to do with shooting, fencing, equestrian and other quasi-military events. Don was now Executive Director of the U.S. Olympic Committee.

I had heard about the Winter Olympics training center in Squaw Valley and thought it was a great idea.

After consulting with Bob Kane, president of the USOC, I talked with Don and sent in my application to be head of the training center. A few weeks later, he offered me the job, which I was delighted to accept. I was back on track.

However, the Squaw Valley setup was to be temporary. The plan was for a permanent training center in Colorado Springs.

I knew I should check with Gwen before making any commitment to move.

"Wanna move?"

"Where to?"

"Colorado Springs."

"Sure."

So, in June 1977 we were on our way to start our new life in Colorado Springs.

Now, you might wonder why Colorado Springs, when at the time the USOC was comfortably and elegantly ensconced on Park Avenue? The reason was pretty much the same as for most decisions.

Dollars.

Thayer Tutt, who ran the Broadmoor Hotel in Colorado Springs, was in charge of the El Poma Foundation. Tutt was a sports leader who was also involved with the National Governing Body for U.S. Figure Skating and felt a world-class arena on or adjacent to his hotel site would be good for business.

The move to Colorado Springs was pretty much assured during lunch between Tutt and Don Miller when Tutt handed Miller a check for a million dollars from the El Poma Foundation.

The deal became even sweeter when the city of Colorado Springs leased the USOC an abandoned NORAD base for a dollar a year.

So there I was, just me—and a secretary—ready to conquer the world. As boring as my job with the selective service had been, that's how frenzied this job would be. Fortunately, I had the experience of running my camp, which had given me some expertise in housing, feeding, and transportation. It would be my responsibility to convert an abandoned NORAD base into the U.S. Olympic Training Center; to oversee its design and construction—certain aspects of which were to prove daunting. For example, the answer to the question, "What's a Training Center?" was left to my definition, which was fine but unexpected.

Construction of the center was also pretty much undefined. We started with a falling-down building over here and a hole in the ground over there. Oh yes, there were barracks running along that line. And then there's this big rock—.

Well, never let it be said that a Mathias walked away from a challenge. My first task was to decide which buildings were usable and which had to be razed. Most of them fell into the latter category, and I would go home at night wondering if the tearing down would ever end so that the building up could begin.

I asked myself more than once: "Was I destroying in order to create—or was I just destroying?" When I read about budgets for developing similar centers today, I marvel how we ever got anything done with the practically nonexistent budget we had to work with. To make things even more frenetic, the U.S. hockey team was scheduled to arrive shortly, and there was absolutely nothing ready for them except some recently repainted rooms.

*Sidebar:* We couldn't know it at the time, but this group of hockey players was the nucleus of the team about which Al Michaels would, on an evening in the winter of 1980, ask a national television audience: "Do you believe in miracles?!"

When the hockey team arrived, we had nothing for them but a bus. We bussed them to restaurants for eating and to the Colorado College arena for skating. I felt so sorry for those kids who thought they would be inaugurating a new practice facility when the only paths they got to blaze were the roads in and out of Colorado Springs.

They were at the USOC Training Center, but the USOC, except for me and my secretary,  was still in its offices in New York. And it was to remain that way until June of 1978.

One of the other problems we faced was dealing with the Balkanized NGBs. The National Governing Body for each sport was its own little fiefdom, and some had their own training facilities, guarded jealously from outside influence. When I suggested we invite the heads of each NGB to the training center site so they could see the potential, it was like we had invited them to a beheading.

But we went ahead anyway. We offered each NGB food and lodging for its athletes along with free office space as an enticement for them to move their headquarters. And had no takers.

But slowly things began moving and started to get organized. We had spent a great deal of time and effort putting together a master plan and a master timetable. Both needed work.

A few isolated NGBs began to come around, and one of the saddest stories of the training center's early years was about a group of 15 girls who made up the U.S. volleyball team. These girls gave up a year and a half of school; left their boyfriends, their homes, their families, their jobs, everything. They gave up everything for their sport and for their country. They trained diligently for over a year. They endured injuries, homesickness and some of the most rigorous training I had ever seen.

They were up at dawn for an eight-mile run in nearby mountains. They came back for breakfast, then, after a short break, went to weight-training sessions. After that, they did windsprints for almost an hour. That brought them to lunchtime. After lunch, they played volleyball for most of the afternoon under the guidance of their coaches.

After dinner, they had brain sessions in which their coaches would instruct them in what-ifs. What if the ball is hit here? What if you've already used two hits and the ball is still in back court?

I could go on and on, but the point is that these girls put their lives into their sport.

When it was time for the 1980 Moscow Summer Olympics to begin, they were ready!

Except for one thing.

President Carter instituted an Olympic boycott, and there would be no Summer Olympics for the American kids in 1980.

These poor girls who had *lived* their sport for so long, with the express purpose of representing their country in the Summer Olympics, were denied.

So were hundreds of others, of course. Bob Koffman, for example, was favored to win the decathlon in 1980, at the peak of his career. Denied.

Not only were the American kids denied their opportunity to compete in 1980, but the Soviet bloc kids were handed the same disappointment in 1984. There has to be a way to keep politics out of sports. Especially since one of the biggest Olympic scandals of all time unfolded in Salt Lake City.

We have accepted the IOC authority as being absolute. Even to the point where Juan Antonio Samaranch is addressed as *Your Excellency*. Come on, give me a break. Your Excellency? Isn't that address reserved for royalty?

Ah, royalty! There, in my opinion, seems to lay much of the problem. IOC officials have become so used to being fawned over and treated like royalty that they have come to believe they *are* special people, no longer subject to the rules and the mores of the real world.

What we need in the Olympic hierarchy, just as we need in our own government, is—term limits!

And why not?

Why can't IOC officials serve for a finite period, then turn over their responsibilities to someone new? Obviously, there would have to be a staggered line of succession, but that would be a simple thing to set up. If anyone wants to undertake this kind of reform, give me a call. I'll be glad to champion the cause.


While I was immersed in preparing the training center for its various activities, I was invited to participate in the Superstars competition. I had always tried to stay in decent shape, so even though I was 49, I figured, why not?

My competitors were guys who were no longer actively competing but had come upon the athletic scene years after me. Listen to these names: Ben Davidson of the Oakland Raiders, John Havlicek of the Boston Celtics, Jim Taylor of the Green Bay Packers and boxers Floyd Patterson and Ingmar Johansson. Dwight Stones, one of the highest of the high jumpers, was also there, but competing in a younger division.

I was able to do okay in everything but, as usual, didn't stand out in anything. The agenda included rowing, tennis, weight lifting, baseball throwing, bike riding, high jumping, the 400 meter run and the obstacle course. My best event was the final one: the obstacle course, in which I won my heat and qualified for the finals the next day. The finals were to be decided by a rerun of the obstacle course.

Even though I won my heat, I pulled a groin muscle and the next day I had to forfeit the race to Ben Davidson because I could barely walk.

During the swimming event, Floyd Patterson was to my right and Ben Davidson was to my left. I was very careful not to say anything to either of these guys to upset them. They were huge! I don't mean in great shape, I just mean huge!

Somebody shot off a gun, and we were off. It was a 50-yard swim, which was two lengths of the pool. I wasn't a great swimmer, so I was in the middle of the pack, but coming back, I saw something really strange. It was a form at the bottom of the pool. My first reaction was that one of the guys was clowning around, so I ignored it and finished my second lap. But when I looked back, it was still down there. So I swam back, dove down and came up with Floyd Patterson.

"What were you doing, kidding around?" I asked him.

"Hell no. I was drowning. I can't swim."

I was going to ask him what he was doing in the pool, but I figured—what's the use?

Some other interesting high—or low—lights from the competition:

- Neither Floyd Patterson nor Ingemar Johansson could jump high enough, nor did they have the arm strength to climb over the wall in the obstacle course.
- Dwight Stones didn't have to use the rope to climb. He almost cleared the wall with a jump.
- Ben Davidson won the competition and was so strong he broke an oar while he was practicing for the rowing event.

After the competition was over, I returned to the training center and my job.

And there was so much to do; so many decisions to be made. The facility was on 23 acres, and everyone—I mean EVERYONE—had his own idea of what should go where and how the land should be used.

Each NGB seemed to have the same mantra, and it went like this:  If we're going to move into your training center, we need our own (fill in the blank): dining hall, dormitory, pool, court, field, limousines, budget, lake, office building, gymnasium.

Each day, each hour it seemed, another question would arise. There were times I envied General Eisenhower. All he had to do was plan the Allied invasion of Normandy.

Which buildings to keep; which to raze?

Of the buildings we would keep, which should be designated for what use?

Which, of those we were keeping, were most suitable for immediate occupancy?

Was the plumbing okay?

What about the wiring?

Should the buildings be painted in lively or somber colors?

Where should the track go?

How long could we get away without swimming and diving facilities?

Above all, and at all times, the overriding question was: "How will we pay for it?"

The training center was *not* a function of the U.S. government.  The entire facility was being funded with private money, and there were more than a few times that we had to stop everything until additional dollars came in to pay for it.

There was agreement on one thing.  The first three priorities *had* to be:

1. An Olympic-sized track
2. An Olympic soccer field
3. A gymnasium with facilities for basketball, volleyball, wrestling, boxing, judo, gymnastics, and a few other sports.

We also needed to find a way to treat the injuries that inevitably would occur—without any funding. We were fortunate to be able to get the services of Bob Beeten, who was a Class A scrounge. I didn't ask and didn't want to know where they came from, but he scrounged treatment tables, alcohol, gauze, tape, even an eye machine. Lots of other stuff began showing up in the old building we had consigned over to Dr. Bob. No one ever asked where it came from, and he never volunteered any information.

We also were able to enlist some volunteer dentists in addition to the MDs that Dr. Bob had brought to us.

Then one day, shrouded in mystery, a Cybex machine showed up. The Cybex measures muscle strength and is also used for equalizing strength in the arms or legs. It's tremendously important in athletic performance. Through obscure means, we also came by a density tank, used for measuring body fat.

Good ol' Doctor Bob had struck again.

One of my proudest moments was when I was able to expand our food service facility by adding three food service chefs who took leaves of absence from their jobs. They were willing to work for what we could afford to pay them, and they improved the quality of our meals by quantum leaps.

Our food service, actually, was pretty good, I thought. You might be able to find a few picky eaters who would argue the point, but I remember when I was competing, the concept of quantity far outweighed quality. I never heard a weightlifter complain the pie crust wasn't flaky enough. Our policy for each meal was to offer two choices of entrees: take all you can eat, eat all you take, and come back as often as you want.

Heavyweight wrestlers made five or six trips to the steam table; girl gymnasts never seemed to eat at all.

Then someone came up with the thought that we weren't feeding the athletes properly. "The training center needs a professional nutritionist to plan the athletes' meals," we were told.

I thought things were fine, but on the other hand, I couldn't see the harm in bringing in a pro to help plan the nutritional aspects of the athletes' training. Up to now, the coaches had been responsible for what their kids ate, and no one seemed to be starving or putting on any excess pounds, but there seemed no harm in adding the nutritionist to our small staff.

So a nutritionist arrived. Since new people feel compelled to do new things, the first new thing she did was to demand that we create little cards showing how many calories were in each serving. How the hell did we know? This was the '70s, way before nutrition content was printed on packages.

Her next move was a beaut. She mandated the number of calories each sport's participant should take in each day—and eliminated second helpings!

Coincidentally, the day she started work was the same day the U.S.A. swimming team came in. Now, I don't know whether you realize how many calories an elite swimmer burns in a day. Try 8,000. Eight thousand calories a day! And that's just to stay even.

These guys, like everyone else, were entitled to only one serving per meal. They began grumbling and complaining how hungry they were almost immediately, and within days their times were skyrocketing and they were losing weight at the rate of a few pounds a day. The team's manager came screaming to me one day: "My guys are starving to death," he said.

I told him: "You're not alone. Write me a letter."

So, with letters from swimming, wrestling, weightlifting, track and field and other managers and coaches, I confronted our crack nutritionist.

"You have to let these kids eat more," I told her.

"Out of the question," she replied. I don't want to be responsible for an Olympic team made up of fat kids."

I could only stare at her.

"Fat kids?" I croaked. "These kids are wasting away and their performance is being affected."

But she was adamant. She wouldn't relent, so finally I had to give her an ultimatum: "My way or the highway." She chose the highway and within weeks we could see the difference. The swimmers' times were plummeting, and the weightlifters' capacities were soaring.

As I said, dollars were always tight, but in an Olympic training center or just in your family life, you don't save money by skimping on what you feed your kids.

Very often, while I would be walking from one venue to another on the training camp grounds, people would stop me and ask if I was Bob Mathias. I would always 'fess up and was glad to let them take their picture with me or sign an autograph book. One day, it hit me: "Who are these people and where are they coming from?"

Wow! I was on to something.

Visitors!

The place was always crawling with visitors. And what did visitors invariably want? Proof that they were there. So I did what was, perhaps, the single-most productive act of my tenure. I opened a gift shop, which started making a profit from day one. We sold T-shirts, hats, pennants, belt buckles, socks, miniature depictions of athletes, you name it. Anything we could stick those five rings on, we did, sold it and made money.


One of the more pleasurable jobs I had as Director of the Training Center was naming things. I named the first two dormitories that were built after Olympic cities and that became a tradition. There were a lot of other buildings we were able to salvage from when the site was a NORAD base. They had never been named, but rather, each had a number designation. It was my privilege to be able to name them, too, after former Olympic cities, such as Helsinki, Oslo, Berlin, Stockholm, London and other cities that had hosted Olympic Games.

Two buildings that were erected years later, however, broke with tradition and were named after my two good friends Don Miller and Bill Simon.

One day, I received a phone call from the local postmaster. "We need your address," he told me.

"I don't think we have one," I told him.

"That's the point," he told me.

"What's the point?" This seemed like another one of those Abbott and Costello-type conversations I seemed to be having more and more frequently.

I heard him take a deep breath, then he started talking to me the way I talked to my kids.

"The Olympic Training Center does not have an address at this time," he said. "Do you understand?"

"Yes."

"Good. I would like you to select an address, that is, a series of numbers, then tell me those numbers. *That* will be your address." Talk about being pedantic—sheesh!

I said: "Okay, now I understand. Can I pick any number I want?"

"Any number you want as long as it's in the 1700 series," he said.

What a no-brainer! "1776," I said without a moment's hesitation.

And so it remained, a number to remind us all of our historic roots, until many years later when the USOC changed the designation to: One Olympic Plaza.

Being the first Director of the USOC Training Center was a fantastic experience.

It was hard work; day after day of hard work and unrelenting deadlines. But I got to deal with some of the most wonderful people in the world.

I should've stayed.

# CHAPTER 30

# On the Move Again

**It was early in the summer of 1983** when I received a call from a representative of President Reagan. The subject was The President's Council on Physical Fitness and Sports.

It seemed that a number of people on the council had contacted Reagan, urging him to form a private sector version of The President's Council, then headed by the late football coach, George Allen. Among those were Dick Kazmier, former Princeton football star; Wilmer (Vinegar Bend) Mizell, a great baseball pitcher of his day and three-term congressman; and a number of board members from some of the nation's best companies.

They had developed a name, The National Fitness Foundation, and a mission. Their goal was to create an organization that would specialize in promoting physical fitness within the business community and show the public ways to keep active, healthy and fit.

It seems they wanted me to come into the foundation as Executive Director.

The National Fitness Foundation came about as a result of a group of men feeling that the President's Council on Physical Fitness wasn't doing the job it was meant to do because it was getting bogged down in governmental debris and low budgets. They felt a private organization would be more effective and, by soliciting funding within the private sector, could better fund itself and broaden the scope of physical fitness throughout the country.

After many months of searching and debate among themselves, they came up with the outline of the new fitness foundation.

Even though this seemed like a marvelous opportunity, I wasn't particularly enthusiastic about leaving my responsibilities with the training center in Colorado Springs. However, the longer it took me to decide, the better the offer kept getting. In the spirit of full disclosure, I should mention that it finally reached a figure that was more than double what I was getting at the training center. So I let my love of a challenge (not to mention a larger paycheck) get the better of me and in November 1983, I gave myself a birthday present by accepting this new position.

I had a painful meeting with Don Miller, who claimed he was sorry to be losing me, but wouldn't hold me back. His parting words were to the effect: "You'll probably have some dealings with the President's Council at first. Watch out for George Allen."


Dick Kazmier had accepted the position as president of the new foundation, and I was looking forward to working with him. It took me a while to wrap up things in Colorado Springs, but in June 1984, Gwen and I were ready to leave the mountains of Colorado and head for the flat plains of Indianapolis.

At the time, the Eli Lilly Endowment was engaged in creating grants in an effort to attract the national governing bodies of many amateur sports to make their headquarters in Indianapolis.

Jim Morris, the head of the Lilly Endowment, promised they would underwrite the building of our headquarters. By way of putting his money where his mouth was, he committed a half-million dollars over five years to the foundation if we would agree to set up shop in Indianapolis. We were off to a great start.

As commitments were made, the cast of characters was expanded. Bill Harris had a company that manufactured fireplace inserts. He was also a co-owner of one of the teams in the now defunct World Football League and a friend of George Allen's. Another friend of George Allen's was Casey Conrad, who had been President of the President's Council on Physical Fitness when Allen came onboard.

Casey left the President's Council and took over the presidency of the Fitness Foundation when Dick Kazmier decided he wouldn't have the time to give to the venture as president but instead would act as an advisor. Casey and I were charged with the responsibility of putting the fitness foundation together and I was surprised when I learned that he would continue living in Sacramento. Gwen and I had already sold our house in Colorado Springs and found a home in Indy.

The people at Indy had contacted me to start looking at some sites they were recommending. Traipsing vacant lots in different parts of Indianapolis was a good way for us to learn about our new hometown as well as checking out some of the locations that were being suggested for the foundation.

During this time of getting settled in Indy, my dealings were with Casey, Kazmier, and a few others. George Allen's name came up once in a while. They said he was busy coaching the Chicago WFL team as well as tending to his duties as head of the President's Council. They also said that, although George would be available as a consultant, it would be a conflict of interest if he were to get involved in the privately funded National Fitness Foundation because of his affiliation with the President's Council, which was publicly funded.


Some time around 600 B.C., Laertius wrote: *"De mortuis nil nisi bonum,"* meaning speak not ill of the dead. That was a fine and noble idea, but, of course, Plutarch had never met George Allen.

Nor had I up to that time, but I knew of him and had admired him as an NFL coach who coined the phrase: "The future is now."

It was of Coach Allen that attorney Edward Bennett Williams, owner of the Washington Redskins once said: "I gave George an unlimited budget, and he overspent it within a month."

I can see how that could have happened.

On the first day of site selection, who was there to lend us his expertise in the fine art of site shopping? George Allen. Where did he come from? I never did find out, but he was there. The rest of us were dressed to tramp through muddy fields. George was wearing a suit and got pissed because his shoes got muddy.

He wasn't satisfied with anything the Lilly people were showing us and, more than once, was asked: "George, what's your role here?" A legitimate question and one he never did answer.

### Gwen Mathias:

*Over the years, Bob has made me crazy by his unwillingness to ever say anything negative about anyone. "It's totally unnatural," I've told him, "Not to ever criticize anyone."*

*Then, when I read what he had to say about George Allen I asked him: "What about your 'say good things only' policy?"*

*He looked to the ceiling, sighed and said: "In George's case, I'm willing to make an exception."*

*Read on.*

After about six months of getting organized in Indy, I got a call from Casey Conrad, who said, in effect: "Too bad about Indy. Hope you're not too inconvenienced."

"What do you mean," I said. "Too bad about Indy? I'm *living* in Indy."

"Oh, haven't you heard? George killed it."

"George who? Killed what?"

You could tell I hadn't been in the loop.

"George Allen killed Indianapolis. Looks like the Foundation's gonna be headquartered in California—in Orange County."

George, by this time, had left the Chicago football team and was coaching another WFL team in Phoenix, the Arizona Wranglers, and was living in his home in the Los Angeles area.

"What?!" You could have heard me in Orange County. "Who the hell does he think he is, and how did he ever get involved in the first place?"

I knew there had to be some mistake, so I continued preparing for the foundation to be headquartered in Indy, a city that was easy to fall in love with.

I heard nothing from anyone for another couple of months, so I figured Casey had gotten some bad information.

Then one morning, I got a call from Charles Luckman, the architect. He told me Coach Allen wanted me to come to his office in Newport Beach, California, to look at some plans for the academy. "Why don't you send them to me?," I said. "I've got a pretty busy schedule."

"Well, Coach Allen would like you to take a look at the site too while you're here."

*Uh-oh.* I figured I'd better get in touch with someone who knew more than I did, so I called Dick Kazmier.

"That's insane," Kazmier said after I explained the conversations I'd been having. "The site is in Indianapolis, not California." Kazmier at least made me feel that I wasn't losing my mind. "Keep in touch with me, and if there's any more talk about that, let me know." I promised I would and, once again, got on with my planning.

But it wouldn't go away. Luckman called again and told me that Allen *needed* me there, and if I couldn't make it, he would just go ahead and start construction without my approval.

I figured it was time to call Kazmier again. After I told him the latest, he said: "Sit tight. I'll get back to you in an hour."

Twenty minutes later, the phone rang, and Kazmier told me he had spoken with the White House, and a letter from the White House legal counsel was going out to Allen that afternoon telling him under no circumstances could he be involved with this program.

"They'll send a copy to you, Bob, so call me if you have any questions," Dick said.

I finally began to relax a little. I had started worrying about the possibility that I had bought a house in Indianapolis and my job was in California—not an easy commute. The next day, I received a copy of the letter telling Allen that: "Under no circumstances can you have anything to do with the National Fitness Foundation—" It went on to explain that to do so would create a conflict of interest for the White House.

"Finally," I thought. "We have that straightened out." But I had been thinking without knowing the real George Allen. It seemed Reagan's lawyers' letter served to convince George that his *real* mission was to get even more involved with the foundation than he had been before.

It was apparent that, to Mr. Allen, instructions from the President of the United States represented a challenge to George Allen's authority.

Things were happening much too quickly to keep up with. For example:

- One day, I received a call from Jim Morris, head of the Eli Lilly Endowment, to tell me he'd had a call from George Allen saying Indianapolis was out and that the foundation was going ahead with plans to set up in Orange County. His question was: "How could something like this happen?"

- Casey Conrad got so mad at Allen that, one day after a conversation with him, he quit his position on the spot.

- The Lilly Endowment cancelled its funding of the program.

- George Allen moved into magnificent offices near his home in Palos Verdes, California, that he claimed would be temporary headquarters for the foundation. Needless to say, all bills for rent, maintenance, furniture, personnel and other items were sent to the National Fitness Foundation while he was spending his time on the President's Council and tending to his own personal interests.

- Without funding from the Eli Lilly Foundation, our organization was just about out of money. "Don't worry about money," said George, who went to Otis Chandler, publisher of the *Los Angeles Times,* to try to get new funding.

- Chandler recommended a fund-raising company in Newport Beach and, at a two-hour meeting of the National Fitness Foundation along with the fund-raisers, it was decided that George, because of his name recognition, should call a list of people to generate the necessary funding. He agreed and then promptly started assigning the names to other staff members, saying; "I don't have time for this."

To make a long story short, but no less painful, I will explain that Gwen and I moved to Laguna Niguel in California's Orange County because George Allen was relentless. He eventually alienated everyone concerned with the foundation and forced them to quit and pursue the other interests with which they were involved. I, on the other hand, had no other pursuits and thought the idea of a NF Academy was a good one.

So we moved and, as always, I concentrated on doing my job.

I began soliciting businesses to send representatives to us so that we could fulfill the mission of the foundation. We would put them through seminars, teaching them how to set up training programs so their personnel could reach a recommended level of fitness. This was moving along nicely, and we had attracted more than 100 companies in less than a few months.

Then George put an end to the seminars.

He refused to participate in any serious fund-raising efforts.

His friends on the NFF board wanted to give him a big salary without him resigning from the President's Council, which turned out to be the last straw as far as I was concerned. On August 31, 1986, to preserve my sanity, I wrote my letter of resignation.


On the surface, it would seem impossible that all this could have been instigated and carried out by a man with absolutely no authority. How he did it was at the time, and remains, a mystery to me. He just had the *chutzpah* and the contacts and was able to get some funding so he tried to pull off almost anything he decided. He flouted authority; all authority—even, as I've mentioned, the authority of the Oval Office. He was arrogant and unfeeling for others, and he was completely self-absorbed.

Of course, these are just my opinions of the man. I have talked with players who played for him, and many have spoken highly of him. So, what can I say? My guess is that while he was a coach, he got used to being an absolute monarch and couldn't cope with the give and take of the business world. He also got used to spending lots of money that wasn't his, trading players, upsetting lives and not thinking about the consequences of his actions.

So, the NFF concept never got off the ground. The idea was a great one, and the NFF would have been a fine, healthy program on a national basis except for the unwelcome and untimely intrusion of one man.

# CHAPTER *31*

# This is a Wrap

**Working with George Allen kind of jaded my outlook** on the world, and I decided I really didn't want to work for anyone anymore. Not the USOC, not any private foundation, not even the President of the United States.

So I went into a sort of semi-retirement that would allow me to pick and choose what *I* wanted to do. I have been asked to become affiliated with some companies whose services and products I respect . . . and enjoy. One of those companies is the Herman Goelitz Candy Company, makers of Jelly Belly candy, of which I am proud to be the honorary chairman of the annual Jelly Belly Golf Tournament held near their offices in northern California each May. As you might know, Jelly Bellies are those miniature jelly beans that are so delicious and have so many *real* tasting flavors. I can't imagine any meeting being as pleasurable as a Goelitz meeting. I just kind of munch my way thorough them and ask a lot of questions to make the meetings last longer.

I am also pleased to sit on the Board of Directors of the Sentinel Family of Mutual Funds in Montpelier, Vermont. "How," you might ask, "did I ever get to sit on the board of a Vermont company?" Well, it *was* a rather circuitous route. Many years ago, I was asked to join the Board of Directors of a mutual fund in Oakland, California—my backyard. That fund was bought by a fund in

Wilmington, Delaware, which was, in turn, bought by a larger fund in Philadelphia. *That* fund merged with Sentinel, so it was basically a financial version of the classic food chain that sends me to a meeting in Montpelier each year.

Making personal appearances has always been enjoyable. I can't possibly remember all the appearances I've made over the years, but the ones I've enjoyed the most were those that were cause-related.

I have represented the Knudsen Division of Kraft-General Foods at the Senior Games in Tempe, Arizona; VISA at their annual decathlon camps; and other companies at similar functions. I have always felt that, if I use a company's product or service, I'm pleased to represent that company. I have never represented a company, nor endorsed, even by implication, any product that I didn't actually use.

And speaking of appearances—do you have any idea how many halls of fame there are in this country? There are hundreds, and I must have been asked to appear at most of them at one time or another.

I've also been honored by a number of halls too. The Olympic Hall of Fame, the Track and Field Hall of Fame, and a dozen or so others.

But one of the most meaningful honors I ever received was on that day when I was told that the place where Sim Innes, Bob Hoegh, Bob Abercrombie and so many of us had played our high school football games and competed in track meets would be renamed Bob Mathias Stadium.

There was something about being honored by my hometown that had a different meaning than the others. Not necessarily *more* meaning; just different, warmer. It also gives me a thrill knowing that Tulare Union High also recently rededicated their gymnasium. It's now called The Sim Innes Gym. I know Sim looks down on it each day and thinks good thoughts about the people of Tulare.


One of the nicest aspects of making personal appearances and being honored by various institutions is the opportunity to meet new people and to renew old acquaintances.

For example, when I attended the Senior Olympics in Tempe, Arizona, I was approached by a face that looked vaguely familiar. "Bob, you old sonofabitch," the face said. Then I recognized the voice as one with whom I had served in the Marines at Camp Pendleton. We spent some time reminiscing about the Corps, and he reminded me of when we were scheduled to ship out to Korea and how lucky we were that the war, or police action, came to an end just shortly before that time.

I'm pleased to say that, since 1948, except for the sad and ill-advised boycott of the Moscow Games of 1980, I have never missed an Olympics. Each Olympic Games gives me the same good feeling all over again. I love to see the world's greatest athletes go head to head against each other to see, for that particular four-year period, who is the best of the best.

One of the things I look forward to most is the certainty that, at each Olympiad, you can count on names you have never heard of to become household words. Think back over the years. Think back to the year Nadia Comeneci came from nowhere to captivate and dominate the world of gymnastics. Think back to Mary Lou Retton, to Mark Spitz, to Katarina Witt, to Greg Louganis.

It's hard to believe that Carl Lewis was once an unknown as was Jackie Joyner-Kersee, Rafer Johnson, Summer Sanders, Picabo Street, Florence Griffith Joyner, Bruce Jenner, and even the great granddaddy of all Olympians, the man upon whom the title "World's Greatest Athlete" was first bestowed, the one and only Jim Thorpe.

These names, obscure and unknown on the Monday of Olympic Life; inscribed on the world's stage in shimmering gold on Tuesday; then taking their place in history for all time on Wednesday.

# CHAPTER 32

# World's Greatest Athlete?

**For obvious reasons, there has been a lot of talk lately** about the 20ᵗʰ Century's greatest athlete. Even *I* have been mentioned by some as a candidate for that honor.

Come on now.

How would you compare an athlete in one sport from one era to an athlete in another sport in a different era? Would someone please tell me just what standards would be used to make a comparison between Bob Mathias and, say, Kareem Abdul-Jabbar?

How would you compare John Havlicek to Steffi Graf?

Or Eric Heiden to Carl Lewis?

Each era produces its greats as does each sport, as does, of course, each sex. If you want to decide who was the greatest baseball player of the '60s, then by all means, compare Mickey Mantle to Willie Mays, Whitey Ford and Yogi Berra.

Early century baseball? Go ahead and choose between Babe Ruth, Lou Gehrig, Ty Cobb, and Tris Speaker. Mid-century? Your candidates are Joe DiMaggio, Ted Williams, and Stan Musial.

But for God's sake, how do you decide who was the greatest *athlete* of the *century*?

Just as an exercise, let's try to decide who was the greatest basketball player of the century. A single name springs to mind, right?

Of course, it was Bevo Francis, who once scored 113 points in
one game for Rio Grande College.

Oh? *Not* Bevo Francis?

Okay, so then how 'bout George Mikan? He was the first 'Big
Man' in the game, and no one dominated basketball as he did before or since. Never heard of him, huh?

Does the name Bob Cousy ring a bell?

A-ha! Yes, finally a familiar name, but surely, you can't say
Cousy was the equal of Michael Jordan.

We-e-e-l-l-l-l, maybe I can.

Earlier in this book, I talked about some of the differences in
athletes from my day to the present. I mentioned training methods, diet, equipment, shoes, sports medicine and some of the other
factors that set one era apart from another. True, I was talking
about track and field at the time, but the same applies to all sports.

Who's to say, if Bob Cousy was a contemporary of Michael
Jordan, he wouldn't be just as good. . .or better. . . than Michael?
Cousy *revolutionized* the game when he played. He led the Boston
Celtics to four consecutive championships (six overall). He was as
unguardable then as Michael was in the '90s.

So, what's the difference between Michael and The Cooz?

Timing.

And television.

If you wanted to see Bob Cousy play basketball, you went to
Boston Garden. If you wanted to see Michael Jordan play, you
could have watched a game on TV. Or watch the news. Or watch
a promo tape. If you watched enough television, you'd have seen
Michael Jordan.

Look, I am not trying to take anything away from Michael.
He is certainly the finest basketball player of his day, and it will be a
long time before we see his likes again. But we *will* see his successor
some day. Maybe Shaquille O'Neal is already the successor. And
maybe then, some aging curmudgeon, who is in his teens today,
will defend Michael Jordan's greatness against some ultra-star of
2033.

Am I making my point?

I realize it's all for fun, this "Who's-the-greatest-athlete-of-the-century" stuff. Frankly, I'm honored that my name should be mentioned along with some of those fine athletes. But let's not take it too seriously. Let's not take the chance of diminishing the glory of yesterday's athletes because they performed in the pre-TV era and there aren't miles and miles of videotape to prove how truly good they were.

There have been suggestions that we anoint the 100 greatest athletes of the century. Okay, so that would soothe 100 egos. But what about the 101st guy? Maybe that would be me. Or Cy Young or Bill Dickey. Or Magic Johnson or Larry Bird. Or Guy LaFleur or Bobby Orr. Or Bart Starr or Jim Brown. Or Eddie Arcaro or Lafitte Pincay. Or Martina Hingis or Martina Navratilova. Or Babe Didrickson or Nancy Lopez. Or Pete Sampras or Rod Laver.

See what I mean?

So, am I just a cranky old guy with a lot of complaints and no solutions? I hope not. Here's my suggestion:

Why not just create a 20th Century Athletes Hall of Fame, and be done with it. Show our respect for hundreds, maybe thousands, of athletes instead of honoring one and dishonoring the rest.

Okay, enough. Maybe the Athlete-of-the-Century *is* a good idea. I just don't happen to think so.


Then, there's the other side of sports. The side that's been so corrupted by money that the word *sport* hardly seems to apply.

So many athletes have made so much money that the locker room has become a gathering place for millionaires. Many of today's athletes are now celebrities first, and athletes second. They seem to feel little or no responsibility to the fans who make their swollen paychecks possible and have made them the celebrities they are.

I referred earlier in this book to the story about Babe Ruth making more money than President Hoover in 1929 and the Babe's justification that he'd had a better year. Today, 70 years later, all professional athletes. . .second and third stringers even. . .make more than the president. Financially, they're all having better years too (if not quite as interesting) as President Clinton.

So, you might be wondering, how did this wide-eyed babe in the woods of the '40s and '50s turn into such a curmudgeon in the '90s. I really didn't. I'm still the same trusting, sweet, generous, courteous guy I was back in Tulare. It's just that life changes us all.

I've met some wonderful people and some not so wonderful. I've led as good a life as most and better than many. I have wonderful memories, a wonderful wife, and wonderful children. That's what I have.

What I don't have is just as wonderful.

I don't have cancer any more.

At my last checkup, I'm delighted to say that I was completely clean of any cancer.

I started this book with cancer, and I'm finishing it without cancer. I just wish everyone in the world could be so lucky.

# AFTERWORD

**I've mentioned a couple of halls of fame in this book.** Some I've been inducted into; others I've just visited. What I'd like to do now is create my own. The Bob Mathias Hall of Fame. Presumptuous? Hey, it's my book. I can do anything I want. And I also wish to put forth my own Hall of Shame.

So that I can end the book on a positive note, I'll put my Hall of Shame first.

Here it comes.

## THE BOB MATHIAS HALL OF SHAME

Originally, my Hall of Shame was very sparsely populated; in fact, there was only one guy - you know who. George Allen.

But, as they say in the NFL, "after further review," I've added to it.

I've added the International Olympic Committee. The IOC needs discipline, new blood, and it needs to consider the shame it has cast upon the thousands of young athletes competing for positions on their nations' Olympic teams. They need someone to model fairness and good. Not greed.

Can I put a *thing*, as opposed to a person, in the hall of shame? I'm going to anyway.

I'm putting *money* in my hall. As they say, it's the root of all evil, and that's certainly true in athletics.

Money is ruining professional sports with multimillion dollar salaries, and it's ruining amateur sports as well. Dave Johnson once told me he felt a little funny when he filed his six-figure income tax form and put down as his employment: Amateur Athlete.

Speaking of money—do we *really* need corporate logos on uniforms that make athletes look like Indy cars? I mean, when will enough be enough?

I hate to pick on Bill Clinton because the poor guy's probably in everyone's Hall of Shame, but here's a guy who screwed up his chances for a legacy as one of our greatest presidents because he was apparently incapable of telling the truth about his indoor sports career.

Here's a broad-based condemnation. I install into my Hall of Shame all those athletes who make tons of money and who are revered by kids throughout the country *and* who refuse to act as positive role models for kids.

Along those same lines, I feel the same contempt for the team owners, managers, coaches, media and sponsors who look the other way when their spoiled athletes act as misfits and sociopaths.

## THE BOB MATHIAS HALL OF FAME

Now let's get on with the good guys; the official, authentic, bona fide, authoritative Bob Mathias Hall of Fame:

Right smack in the middle of the entranceway, so no one can miss her, goes **Gwen Mathias**. The English language lacks sufficient superlatives to do her justice, so I'll just say she's been, and continues to be, the best wife a man could ever have.

Next come the kids, Romel, Megan, Marissa, Reiner and Alyse followed by their kids, Lucas and Alex Gruenther, Chance Hildreth, Sara, Eza and Max Solomon, Haven, Jordan and Elijah Halstead and Crystal Mathias.

Before I get to people, I'd like to mention a couple of categories of people. Maybe they're not all Hall of Famers, but they're all worth a mention in this book—*all* the young men and women in multi-event competition; the heptathlon, pentathlon, and the decathlon.

And I'll also include every athlete who competes for the U.S.A. in the Olympics. Each one of them has the potential to bring tears to our eyes as the "Star-Spangled Banner" is played.

**Glen Morris, Milt Campbell, Rafer Johnson, Bill Toomey, Bruce Jenner** and **Dan O'Brien**—the American gold medalists in the decathlon. Each one proved he was the world's greatest athlete at the time in his life when it counted.

And I should mention **Dave Johnson**, who, in 1992, turned in one of the gutsiest performances in the decathlon I've ever seen. Dave competed with a stress fracture in his foot, yet won the bronze medal when he should have been in an orthopedist's office.

The guy who started the U.S. dominance in the decathlon, back in 1912—a man I actually had the privilege of meeting—the great **Jim Thorpe**: in my opinion the greatest all-around athlete who ever lived on this planet. Given today's training methods, equipment, diet and coaching, Thorpe would not only win the Olympic decathlon and just about any other event he entered, he would also be a standout in the NFL and Major League Baseball.

The name **Virgil Jackson** must be near the entrance of the hall. If it hadn't been for Coach Jackson's wisdom and constant encouragement, I'd probably be a doctor today.

Not that he needs my accolades, but I'm including **Ted Williams**, arguably the greatest hitter of all-time, even if he thinks hitting a home run is tougher than setting a new world record in track.

**Tiger Woods** was a Stanford guy, as was **John Elway, Frankie Albert, Gary Kerkorian, John Brodie, Dick Berg, Jim Plunkett**, and so many other great quarterbacks.

How can an athletic Hall of Fame be complete without The Great Levitator, **Michael Jordan**? He could have been a great long jumper, high jumper, and maybe the greatest ever decathlete.

In the decathlon mode, I hereby install **John Bennett** in my Hall of Fame. John was head of VISA's magnificent program that funded the training and coaching (and helped in many other ways), of American kids competing in the decathlon. If it weren't for John's efforts, it's unlikely America's decathlon program would have come back as far as it has in the past two Olympics.

And how could we talk of the decathlon without bringing up the guru of the decathlon—**Frank Zarnowski**?! Zeke has encyclopedic knowledge of the event and is everyone's reference point when the event is discussed.

Mara and Samara! **Harry Mara** and **Fred Samara**, America's Olympic Decathlon coaches have been instrumental in producing medals for the U.S. since 1992. **Sam Adams** also deserves to be in this group, but I couldn't pass up the Mara and Samara line.

Then there's **Arnold Schwarzenegger**, not an athlete in the sense of those mentioned above, but a former world champion bodybuilder. Arnold is also an actor who has given me a great deal of pleasure with his ability to portray violence with his tongue firmly in his cheek.

And speaking of actors, I would like to recognize those who do action films and, especially, their stunt doubles. They add another dimension of excitement to the movies.

President **Gerald Ford** also goes into my Hall of Fame. He was an All-American football player at the University of Michigan, a great legislator and a man who, through circumstances beyond his control, found himself at the seat of world power at one of the most trying times in American history. He was a great friend and, in my opinion, a great president.

**Jack Kemp**, whether he ever runs for president or not, was an outstanding legislator and one of the best quarterbacks the NFL has ever known.

**Ronald Reagan**, the "Gipper," the governor, the president.

**Wilmer "Vinegar Bend" Mizell** was the only congressman in the history of the republic who was required to pitch with his "other" arm in baseball games between House Democrats and Republicans.

My guys! **Bob Hoegh, Sim Innes, Bob Abercrombie, Dane Sturgeon, John Lampe, Dick Sturgeon, Dick Bramer** and other members of Tulare Union High teams that made me look good.

Last, but certainly not least in the Mathias Hall of Fame, come **Doctors Pinto**, **David Tate**, **Don Goffinet** and **Willard Fee** at the Stanford Medical Center. That's not to overlook all those thousands of doctors and researchers who have labored in obscurity since the beginning of time, to treat and find cures for diseases such as cancer, polio and the hundreds of other diseases we no longer have to worry about . . . because they did.

# Career Timeline

| | |
|---|---|
| Nov. 17 1930 | Bob Mathias born, second of four children to Dr. Charles and Lillian Mathias |
| June, 1948 | Enters first decathlon, Los Angeles, wins |
| June, 1948 | Wins Olympic trial in decathlon |
| Aug. 6, 1948 | Wins first Olympic gold medal in decathlon (London) |
| Sept. 1948-June 1949 | Attends Kiskiminetas Prep, (Saltsburg, PA) |
| Sept. 1949 | Enters Stanford University |
| Jan. 1, 1951 | Plays fullback for Stanford vs. Illinois in Rose Bowl |
| Summer, 1951 | Spends summer at U.S. Marine Corps boot camp, Camp Pendleton, CA |
| Aug. 1952 | Wins second straight Olympic gold medal in decathlon (Helsinki) |
| May 1953 | Graduates from Stanford |
| Dec. 1953-July 1954 | Mathlon Productions, Stars in movie, *The Bob Mathias Story* |
| July 1954-Aug. 1956 | U.S. Marines, Quantico, VA, Camp Pendleton, CA |
| Oct. 1956-Apr 1958 | Batjac Productions, actor |
| Apr. 1958-Nov. 1958 | Unemployed |
| Nov. 1858-Jan. 1959 | Northstar Productions, actor |
| Jan. 1959-July 1959 | George A. Fuller Construction |
| July 1959-Dec. 1960 | United Artists, actor |
| Jan. 1961-Jan. 1962 | Unemployed |

| | |
|---|---|
| Jan. 1962-<br>June 1978 | Opens Bob Mathias Sierra Boys Camp |
| Jan. 3, 1967-<br>Jan. 3 1975 | U.S. Congress |
| June 6, 1975-<br>Aug. 11, 1975 | U.S. Govt. Deputy Director of Selective Service System |
| Aug. 1975-<br>Dec. 1975 | President Ford's Presidential Finance Committee |
| Jan. 1976-<br>Jan. 1977 | President's Council on Physical Fitness |
| June 1977-<br>Nov. 1983 | Director, U.S. Olympic Training Center, Colorado Springs |
| Nov. 1983-<br>Aug. 1986 | Exec. Director, National Fitness Foundation |
| Aug. 1986- | President, Bob Mathias, Inc. |